OPPOSING
VIEWPOINTS®
SERIES

D0796594

Big Pharma and Drug Pricing

Other Books of Related Interest

Opposing Viewpoints Series

Alternative Medicine
Corporate Social Responsibility
The Pharmaceutical Industry
Universal Health Care

At Issue Series

Corporate Corruption
Poverty in America
Prescription Drugs
The Wealth Divide

Current Controversies Series

Health Care
Prescription Drugs
Resistant Infections
Vaccines

> "Congress shall make no law … abridging the freedom of speech, or of the press."

First Amendment to the US Constitution

The basic foundation of our democracy is the First Amendment guarantee of freedom of expression. The Opposing Viewpoints series is dedicated to the concept of this basic freedom and the idea that it is more important to practice it than to enshrine it.

SERIES

Big Pharma and Drug Pricing

Pete Schauer, Book Editor

GREENHAVEN
PUBLISHING

Published in 2018 by Greenhaven Publishing, LLC
353 3rd Avenue, Suite 255, New York, NY 10010

Articles in Greenhaven Publishing anthologies are often edited for length to meet page
requirements. In addition, original titles of these works are changed to clearly present
the main thesis and to explicitly indicate the author's opinion. Every effort is made to
ensure that Greenhaven Publishing accurately reflects the original intent of the authors.
Every effort has been made to trace the owners of the copyrighted material.

Cover image: LUCAS TRIEB/AFP/Getty Images

Library of Congress Cataloging-in-Publication Data

Names: Schauer, Peter J., editor.
Title: Big pharma and drug pricing / Pete Schauer, book editor.
Description: New York : Greenhaven Publishing, 2018. | Series: Opposing
  viewpoints | Audience: Grade 9 to 12. | Includes bibliographical
  references and index.
Identifiers: LCCN 2017036789| ISBN 9781534501768 (library bound) | ISBN
  9781534501829 (pbk.)
Subjects: LCSH: Drugs—Prices—United States—Juvenile literature. |
  Prescription pricing—United States—Juvenile literature. | Pharmaceutical
  industry—United States—Juvenile literature. | Drugs—United States—Cost
  control—Juvenile literature.
Classification: LCC HD9665.4 .S33 2018 | DDC 338.4/361510973—dc23
LC record available at https://lccn.loc.gov/2017036789

Manufactured in the United States of America

Website: http://greenhavenpublishing.com

Contents

Chapter 1: Why Are Prescription Drugs So Expensive?

Chapter 2: Why Don't Insurance Companies Cover All Prescription Drugs?

Chapter 3: What Are the Ethics Behind Charging Astronomical Prices for Prescription Drugs?

Chapter 4: Will We See Legislative Changes to the Way Drugs Are Priced?

The Importance of Opposing Viewpoints

Perhaps every generation experiences a period in time in which the populace seems especially polarized, starkly divided on the important issues of the day and gravitating toward the far ends of the political spectrum and away from a consensus-facilitating middle ground. The world that today's students are growing up in and that they will soon enter into as active and engaged citizens is deeply fragmented in just this way. Issues relating to terrorism, immigration, women's rights, minority rights, race relations, health care, taxation, wealth and poverty, the environment, policing, military intervention, the proper role of government—in some ways, perennial issues that are freshly and uniquely urgent and vital with each new generation—are currently roiling the world.

If we are to foster a knowledgeable, responsible, active, and engaged citizenry among today's youth, we must provide them with the intellectual, interpretive, and critical-thinking tools and experience necessary to make sense of the world around them and of the all-important debates and arguments that inform it. After all, the outcome of these debates will in large measure determine the future course, prospects, and outcomes of the world and its peoples, particularly its youth. If they are to become successful members of society and productive and informed citizens, students need to learn how to evaluate the strengths and weaknesses of someone else's arguments, how to sift fact from opinion and fallacy, and how to test the relative merits and validity of their own opinions against the known facts and the best possible available information. The landmark series Opposing Viewpoints has been providing students with just such critical-thinking skills and exposure to the debates surrounding society's most urgent contemporary issues for many years, and it continues to serve this essential role with undiminished commitment, care, and rigor.

The key to the series's success in achieving its goal of sharpening students' critical-thinking and analytic skills resides in its title—

Opposing Viewpoints. In every intriguing, compelling, and engaging volume of this series, readers are presented with the widest possible spectrum of distinct viewpoints, expert opinions, and informed argumentation and commentary, supplied by some of today's leading academics, thinkers, analysts, politicians, policy makers, economists, activists, change agents, and advocates. Every opinion and argument anthologized here is presented objectively and accorded respect. There is no editorializing in any introductory text or in the arrangement and order of the pieces. No piece is included as a "straw man," an easy ideological target for cheap point-scoring. As wide and inclusive a range of viewpoints as possible is offered, with no privileging of one particular political ideology or cultural perspective over another. It is left to each individual reader to evaluate the relative merits of each argument— as he or she sees it, and with the use of ever-growing critical-thinking skills—and grapple with his or her own assumptions, beliefs, and perspectives to determine how convincing or successful any given argument is and how the reader's own stance on the issue may be modified or altered in response to it.

This process is facilitated and supported by volume, chapter, and selection introductions that provide readers with the essential context they need to begin engaging with the spotlighted issues, with the debates surrounding them, and with their own perhaps shifting or nascent opinions on them. In addition, guided reading and discussion questions encourage readers to determine the authors' point of view and purpose, interrogate and analyze the various arguments and their rhetoric and structure, evaluate the arguments' strengths and weaknesses, test their claims against available facts and evidence, judge the validity of the reasoning, and bring into clearer, sharper focus the reader's own beliefs and conclusions and how they may differ from or align with those in the collection or those of their classmates.

Research has shown that reading comprehension skills improve dramatically when students are provided with compelling, intriguing, and relevant "discussable" texts. The subject matter of these collections could not be more compelling, intriguing, or urgently relevant to today's students and the world they are poised to inherit. The anthologized articles and the reading and discussion questions that are included with them also provide the basis for stimulating, lively, and passionate classroom debates. Students who are compelled to anticipate objections to their own argument and identify the flaws in those of an opponent read more carefully, think more critically, and steep themselves in relevant context, facts, and information more thoroughly. In short, using discussable text of the kind provided by every single volume in the Opposing Viewpoints series encourages close reading, facilitates reading comprehension, fosters research, strengthens critical thinking, and greatly enlivens and energizes classroom discussion and participation. The entire learning process is deepened, extended, and strengthened.

For all of these reasons, Opposing Viewpoints continues to be exactly the right resource at exactly the right time—when we most need to provide readers with the critical-thinking tools and skills that will not only serve them well in school but also in their careers and their daily lives as decision-making family members, community members, and citizens. This series encourages respectful engagement with and analysis of opposing viewpoints and fosters a resulting increase in the strength and rigor of one's own opinions and stances. As such, it helps make readers "future ready," and that readiness will pay rich dividends for the readers themselves, for the citizenry, for our society, and for the world at large.

Introduction

> "Increasingly, drug companies have figured out ways to bring to market a variety of drugs with minimal to no investment in clinical research, and almost no risk. … [D]espite growing recognition of the problem and the consequences to the cost of healthcare in the U.S. from excess drug costs, little has happened legislatively to curb these abuses."
>
> —"How Big Pharma Might Be Cut Down to Size," by Robert Pearl, M.D., Forbes, May 11, 2017

Prescription drugs—and the costs associated with them—have long been a hot topic in the US, or at least since the earliest 2000's when it was revealed that America had some of the highest-priced prescription drugs in the world; more expensive than India, the United Kingdom, or Canada. The average US citizen is most likely aware that prescription drug costs are extremely high in America, but it is primarily those who depend on these drugs day in and day out who have a better understanding of why costs for prescriptions are so expensive. Consumers who are constantly paying for prescriptions have seen first-hand the relationships and struggles between pharmaceutical manufacturers, insurance companies, physicians, and pharmacists.

The purpose of *Opposing Viewpoints: Big Pharma and Drug Pricing* is to educate everyone—from the average American to the daily prescription user—about the reasons for high drug costs in the US and what, if anything, can be done to improve what is one of the largest issues our country faces today.

The first chapter introduces readers to the pharmaceutical landscape in America and immediately addresses the looming question of why prescription drugs are so expensive. It specifically focuses on the drug manufacturers themselves and the fact that they are able to set their own prices, which allows for high costs. The chapter also discusses how the US government has allowed these large pharmaceutical companies to set the market in terms of price for the drugs and how important of a role the higher education landscape plays in the pharmaceutical industry.

Insurance companies also play a large role in the pharmaceutical industry as well. Along those lines, the next chapter aims to explain another major issue with the US health care system when it comes to prescription drug coverage, going in depth as to why insurance companies do not cover all prescription drugs. The US government again comes into play, as readers learn about the monopolies and partnerships between government parties and pharmaceutical companies to help maintain campaign and political funds via high priced medications. The second chapter also analyzes what specific types of medications are contributing to soaring prices and what employers of large corporations can do to help reduce prescription drug costs.

Once readers have a strong understanding of how drug manufacturers and insurance companies influence the high cost of prescriptions, they can develop their own decision on if charging these types of enormous prices is ethical or not, which is the subject of the third chapter. As the X-factor of this book, chapter 3 is an eye opener in terms of seeing how the United States stacks up in drug coverage and pricing in comparison to other countries around the world. Viewpoints from doctors, consumers, and even the American Association of Retired Persons (AARP) examine both sides of the ethical boundary and ultimately leave readers to decide which side of the fence they are on when it comes to pharmaceutical pricing ethics.

The text concludes in chapter 4 by looking ahead for what may come down the road in the pharmaceutical industry. Viewpoints focus on what will ultimately be the key to lowering prices: the US government. Will we see legislative change to the way drugs are priced, or will the government continue to pad its own agenda and stand pat against the war on high priced drugs? That is the question that both readers and consumers will be asking themselves, but chapter 4 does present ideas and suggestions on how the government can step in and help to address the issue, and one viewpoint even goes as far as to say that the government isn't to blame for this current issue that we are facing in America. Regardless, prescription drug prices continue to escalate, and multiple parties must work together to help see change.

OPPOSING
VIEWPOINTS®
SERIES

CHAPTER 1

Why Are Prescription Drugs So Expensive?

Chapter Preface

Why are prescription drugs so expensive? It is the age old question that has been baffling consumers for years and the same question that large pharmaceutical companies have had to combat. Throughout the course of this chapter, readers will hear two different vantage points regarding the high cost of prescription drugs in America. One perspective is from the consumer, who must pay these high costs to maintain their health—or stay alive. From their perspective, especially for those who have been taking prescription medications for a long time, the costs only continue to increase, despite the introduction of new coverages and benefits. Consumers always hear how big the pharmaceutical industry is, and as they continue to pay these whopping costs each month, it is easy to see why.

The other perspective comes from the drug companies themselves, which are charging astronomical amounts for medicines that people depend on. The drug companies claim to have their reasons for justifying the high costs of drugs, including all of the funding that is needed for research and development of new medications. It is also possible that consumers' perception of price has changed over the years. The old, cheap copays that consumers used to pay actually shielded them from knowing the true price of the drug, and with out-of-pocket expenses becoming a recurring theme in this day and age, consumers are now paying more than they ever did for drugs despite the fact that the actual cost of the drug may have declined.

But the question remains: Why are prescription drugs so much more expensive in the United States? When consumers see significantly lower prices for comparable medications in Canada and other countries, it is difficult for pharmaceutical companies to justify their sky-high prices.

This chapter will serve as a foundation for the rest of the resource, as it is important to understand why prescription medications are so expensive in the United States before one can understand bigger picture topics, like why insurance companies only cover certain prescriptions or the ethics behind charging astronomical prices for drugs. By the end of this chapter, readers will have a strong understanding of the pharmaceutical landscape in America, ultimately gaining an understanding of why prescriptions are so expensive in this country.

> *"A jump in the number of new expensive drugs hitting the market — along with moves by drugmakers like Turing to raise the price on older and generic drugs — have helped make prescription drugs the fastest-growing segment of the nation's health care tab."*

The Truth Behind the High Costs of Prescription Drugs

Julie Appleby

In the following viewpoint, Julie Appleby educates readers on the question on the minds of many people: How are drug prices set in the US? Appleby bases her topic off of Turing Pharmaceuticals' whopping 5,000 percent price hike on Daraprim, a common drug used to treat toxoplasmosis. Appleby discusses both the positives and negatives of high drug costs; the positives being that revenue driven from prescription drug costs gets reinvested back into research, while the negatives are that citizens can't afford the high drug costs, and the continuous fluctuating costs of drugs just isn't fair to consumers. Appleby reports on the health care law's implementation, health care treatments and costs, trends in health insurance, and policy affecting hospitals and other medical providers for Kaiser Health News.

"Why Some Prescription Drugs Are So Expensive," by Julie Appleby, Kaiser Health News, October 19, 2015.

As you read, consider the following questions:

1. What percent of all health care spending do prescription drugs account for?
2. Which two Democratic presidential candidates were mentioned as opposing high drug costs?
3. What is the name of the drug that was mentioned as given for non-small cell lung cancer?

When Turing Pharmaceuticals raised the price of an older generic drug by more than 5,000 percent last month, the move sparked a public outcry. How, critics wondered, could a firm charge $13.50 a pill for a treatment for a parasitic infection one day and $750 the next?

The criticism led Turing's unapologetic CEO to say he'd pare back the increase – although no new price has yet been named – and the New York attorney general has launched an antitrust investigation. The outcry has again focused attention on how drug prices are set in the United States. Aside from some limited government control in the veterans health care system and Medicaid, prices are generally shaped by what the market will bear.

A jump in the number of new expensive drugs hitting the market — along with moves by drugmakers like Turing to raise the price on older and generic drugs — have helped make prescription drugs the fastest-growing segment of the nation's health care tab. Prescription drugs account for about 10 percent of all health care spending. Two ideas for curbing that spending surface every time a price spike renews interest in drug costs: Letting consumers buy products from other countries with lower prices set by government controls, and allowing Medicare administrators to negotiate drug prices, from which they are currently barred.

Both proposals are getting an airing in Washington and on the campaign trail, pushed by Democratic presidential candidates Hillary Clinton and Bernie Sanders. Opposition is heavy, particularly to Medicare negotiations, and neither is likely to gain much traction.

Drugmakers and some economists argue that price controls or other efforts aimed at slowing spending by targeting profits mean cutting money that could go toward developing the next new cure. Because many pharmaceutical companies spend more on marketing than research, some lawmakers counter that the industry could spend less on promoting its products. Health insurers, in turn, blame drugmakers for high prices, even as they shift more cost to consumers, who then fear they won't be able to afford their medications.

Aside from the perennial ideas, what else is being tried to combat rising prices or at least bring some relief to consumers?

1) Disclose drug development costs

Lawmakers in several states, including New York, Pennsylvania and Massachusetts, have introduced "transparency" measures that would force drug companies to provide details on how much they spend researching, making and advertising their products. Proponents say public disclosure would force companies to justify their pricing. Skeptics say disclosure alone may not be enough, so some proposals go further. Massachusetts, for example, would gather price information on a set of drugs deemed critical to the state—and create a commission that could set prices for drugs deemed too costly. None of the measures have passed. On the national front, Clinton proposes to require companies that benefit from federal investment in basic science research to invest a certain amount of their own revenue in research and development.

Some economists say the state and national effort is misguided. Research costs aren't a good way to justify a drug's ultimate price, they say. Looking at a single drug produced by a company ignores the huge amounts spent on other products that failed but still provided clues for the product that did succeed. And, some economists say, such rules might simply foster more money spent on research that isn't needed.

2) Cap consumer copayments

The growing number of insurers placing certain high-cost drugs in categories in which consumers have to pay a percentage of the cost—often upward of 30 percent—has caught the attention of lawmakers in a handful of states, including Montana, California and Delaware. They've passed laws capping the amount insured consumers must pay at the pharmacy counter as their share of a drug's cost. The pocketbook cost for patients is still high, ranging from $100 a month to $250, depending on the state. Still, that's less than what consumers currently pay for some drugs in many health insurance plans. While such laws could help consumers with out-of-pocket costs, it doesn't affect the underlying price of those drugs. Critics say in some cases, such rules may encourage greater use of costly drugs for which there are less expensive alternatives.

3) Pay up if the product delivers

A drug's price should reflect its effectiveness, according to new efforts under way. Benefit manager Express Scripts, for example, next year will pay varying amounts for a small set of oncology drugs based on how well the products perform on different types of cancer. The plan will target drugs that work well on one type of cancer—based on clinical data submitted by drugmakers to the Food and Drug Administration—but are less effective against other types. For instance, the drug Tarceva, when given for non-small cell lung cancer, prolongs life an average of 5.2 months, a big advance for lung cancer treatments, said Steve Miller, senior vice president and chief medical officer at Express Scripts. But, when the $6,200-a-month drug is used to treat pancreatic cancer, it prolongs life an average of only 12 days. Under the new program, insurers would pay the drugmaker less when the treatment is given to pancreatic cancer patients. "We're trying to slow the rising cost of treating cancer," said Miller, who said if it works with a small set of cancer drugs, the firm may look to expand to other types of treatments. Variations on the theme are being explored by others, including Novartis, which has said it is in talks with insurers about varying payments based on how well its new heart drug prevents hospitalizations. Both pricing plans face obstacles, such as how to set the right price and how to determine if it was the drug—or something else—that led to fewer hospitalizations.

Meanwhile, consumer groups are cautious, saying such "pay-for-value" ideas hold promise, but only if patients aren't kept from needed medicines.

These are just three of the proposals being weighed as solutions to combat rising drug prices, but none of them will provide a quick fix.

Price spikes aren't the only reason the drug industry is under scrutiny. Experts advocate for more education for both doctors and consumers; specifically, they say comparative information about drugs and costs should be more widely available.

Doctors often don't know how much a particular treatment costs, which is "one of the reasons why [increased] competition isn't a big enough factor," said Joseph Antos of the American Enterprise Institute. "I hope this concern about high drug prices would translate into a stronger push for getting beyond platitudes about creating informed consumers and actually doing it."

Unbiased, medical information about the use of new drugs needs to be easier to get as well, said Jerry Avorn, a professor of medicine at Harvard. That's particularly true with expensive new products like injectable cholesterol control medications that hit the market this summer. Aside from some patients with a rare form of hereditary high cholesterol, the $14,000-a-year drugs were approved by the FDA only for those patients for whom a less expensive class of drugs, called statins, have been unable to control their "bad" cholesterol levels.

"We've got to get word out to doctors, 'Here's this new class of drugs and here's who needs it and here's who doesn't,'" Avorn said. He has long supported "academic detailing," which sends representatives to doctor offices with such detailed information. "It's important to get to doctors with the best evidence, so they're not just relying on the [pharmaceutical] sales representative."

> *"Prescription drugs on average cost more than twice as much in the U.S. as in other developed nations. That's mostly due to name-brand drugs. They represent 10 percent of all prescriptions but account for almost three-quarters of the total amount spent on drugs in the U.S. Their prices have doubled in the past five years."*

Higher Education Plays an Important Role in the Pharma Industry

Annie Waldman

In the following excerpted viewpoint, Annie Waldman examines the recent trend of large pharmaceutical companies enlisting the help of some of the smartest professors in the country to help justify the extremely high price of prescription drugs. Waldman details that these professors—who in some cases serve on the board for the drug companies—are writing research journals that state the benefits of particular drugs, thus essentially helping to sell lawmakers and consumers on the product. Waldman is a reporter covering education for ProPublica. She recently graduated with honors from the dual masters program at Columbia's School of International and Public Affairs and the School of Journalism.

"Big Pharma Quietly Enlists Leading Professors to Justify $1,000-Per-Day Drugs," by Annie Waldman, Pro Publica Inc., February 23, 2017. Reprinted by permission.

As you read, consider the following questions:

1. What virus saw the price of the treatments range from $40,000 to $94,000?
2. How much money did big pharma spend while successfully defeating a California referendum that would have controlled the prices of both generic and name-brand drugs?
3. What does the acronym "JAMA" stand for?

Over the last three years, pharmaceutical companies have mounted a public relations blitz to tout new cures for the hepatitis C virus and persuade insurers, including government programs such as Medicare and Medicaid, to cover the costs. That isn't an easy sell, because the price of the treatments ranges from $40,000 to $94,000 — or, because the treatments take three months, as much as $1,000 per day.

To persuade payers and the public, the industry has deployed a potent new ally, a company whose marquee figures are leading economists and health care experts at the nation's top universities. The company, Precision Health Economics, consults for three leading makers of new hepatitis C treatments: Gilead, Bristol-Myers Squibb, and AbbVie. When AbbVie funded a special issue of the American Journal of Managed Care on hepatitis C research, current or former associates of Precision Health Economics wrote half of the issue. A Stanford professor who had previously consulted for the firm served as guest editor-in-chief.

At a congressional briefing last May on hepatitis C, three of the four panelists were current or former Precision Health Economics consultants. One was the firm's co-founder, Darius Lakdawalla, a University of Southern California professor.

"The returns to society actually exist even at the high prices," Lakdawalla assured the audience of congressional staffers and health policymakers. "Some people who are just looking at the problem as a pure cost-effectiveness problem said some of these prices in some ways are too low."

Even as drug prices have come under fierce attack by everyone from consumer advocates to President Donald Trump, insurers and public health programs have kept right on shelling out billions for the new hepatitis C treatments, just as Precision Health Economics' experts have urged them. With a battle looming between the industry and Trump, who has accused manufacturers of "getting away with murder" and vowed to "bring down" prices, the prestige and credibility of the distinguished academics who moonlight for Precision Health Economics could play a crucial role in the industry's multipronged push to sway public and congressional opinion.

While collaboration between higher education and industry is hardly unusual, the professors at Precision Health Economics have taken it to the next level, sharpening the conflicts between their scholarly and commercial roles, which they don't always disclose. Their activities illustrate the growing influence of academics-for-hire in shaping the national debate on issues from climate change to antitrust policy, which ultimately affect the quality of life and the household budgets of ordinary Americans—including what they pay for critical medications.

The pharmaceutical industry is digging in, with one of its trade groups raising an additional $100 million for its "war chest." For years, it has spent millions of dollars lobbying politicians, hoping to enlist their support on a wide range of legislation. It has similarly wooed doctors, seeking to influence what they research, teach and prescribe. Now, it's courting health economists.

"This is just an extension of the way that the drug industry has been involved in every phase of medical education and medical research," said Harvard Medical School professor Eric G. Campbell, who studies medical conflicts of interest. "They are using this group of economists it appears to provide data in high-profile journals to have a positive impact on policy."

The firm participates in many aspects of a drug's launch, both advising on "pricing strategies" and then demonstrating the value of a drug once it comes on the market, according to its brochure. "Led by professors at elite research universities," the group boasts of a range of valuable services it has delivered to clients, including generating "academic publications in the world's leading research journals" and helping to lead "formal public debates in prestigious, closely watched forums."

Precision Health Economics may be well-positioned to influence the Trump administration. Tomas Philipson, an economist at the University of Chicago and the third co-founder of Precision Health Economics, reportedly served briefly as a senior health care adviser for the Trump transition team. He did not respond to requests for comment. Dr. Scott Gottlieb, reported to be a candidate for commissioner of the Food and Drug Administration, is a clinical assistant professor at New York University School of Medicine and a former "academic affiliate" of Precision Health Economics, according to its website.

Although it's hard to gauge the firm's precise impact, associates of Precision Health Economics have often waded into the political fray. Last fall, big pharma spent more than $100 million successfully defeating a California referendum that would have controlled the prices of both generic and name-brand drugs. Testifying in September at a state Senate hearing on a generic drug, co-founder Goldman steered the discussion to name-brand drugs, such as the hepatitis C treatments, arguing that their prices should not be regulated.

"We have to ensure access to future innovation, and that's going to require some recognition that if someone develops an innovative drug, they're going to charge a lot for it," Goldman said.

Prescription drugs on average cost more than twice as much in the U.S. as in other developed nations. That's mostly due to name-brand drugs. They represent 10 percent of all prescriptions but account for almost three-quarters of the total amount spent on drugs in the U.S. Their prices have doubled in the past five years.

The U.S. grants drugmakers several years of market exclusivity for their products and remains one of the only industrialized countries that allows them to set their own prices. These protections have allowed the pharmaceutical industry to become one of the economy's most profitable sectors, with margins double those of the auto and petroleum industries.

To justify the value of expensive drugs, the professors affiliated with Precision Health Economics rely on complicated economic models that purport to quantify the net social benefits that the drugs will create.

For one industry-funded hepatitis C study, Lakdawalla and nine co-authors, including three pharmaceutical company researchers, subtracted the costs of the treatment from the estimated dollar value of testing all patients and saving all livers and lives. By testing and treating all patients now, they concluded, society would gain $824 billion over 20 years.

Critics have at times questioned the assumptions underlying the consultants' economic models, such as the choice of patient populations, and suggested that some of their findings tilt toward their industry clients. For example, some have tried and failed to reproduce their results justifying the value of cancer treatments.

Precision Health Economics allows drugmakers to review articles by its academics prior to publication in academic journals, said a former business development manager of the consulting group. Such prior review is controversial in higher education because it can be seen as impinging on academic freedom.

"Like other standard consulting projects, you can't publish unless you get permission from the company," the former employee said. Carolyn Harley, senior vice president and general manager of the firm, said that pre-publication review was not company policy, but "in some cases, client contracts provide them the opportunity for review and comment before submission."

"I have never published anything that I am not comfortable with or prepared to defend, nor have I ever been asked to," said Lakdawalla about his firm's research.

Goldman says the firm's research is independent, and its clients don't influence its findings. "From my perspective it's very clear: I say things that piss off my sponsors, I say things that piss off the detractors," he told ProPublica. "People are coming to us because they have an interest in sponsoring the research that's generated. These are our ideas. This is how you get your ideas recognized."

He said his consulting work does not involve setting prices of specific drugs, and his academic research focuses only on categories of drugs, rather than on particular brands.

The professors' disclosure of their ties to the firm and to the pharmaceutical industry in scholarly articles is inconsistent: sometimes extensive, sometimes scanty. Members of Precision Health tend to reveal less about their paid work in blogs, public forums like conferences, and legislative testimony. At the Capitol Hill briefing last May on hepatitis C drugs, Lakdawalla didn't mention his affiliation with Precision Health Economics, though it was listed in the journal issue, which was provided to attendees.

"Conflicts are always a concern, which is why it is important to be transparent about study methods—that way they can be scrutinized and debated in the academic literature," said Lakdawalla, adding that he has disclosed his ties to the firm in at least 33 publications over the past three years.

Goldman said he and other academics at Precision Health Economics disclose their ties whenever appropriate, but typically journal editors and conference sponsors decide how to make that information available. "I wear two hats," Goldman said in an interview. "And I try to reveal what that might mean in terms of perceived conflict of interest."

The issues at stake aren't just academic. Goldman says that pharmaceutical companies need to reap financial rewards from the enormous time and expense they invest in developing better medical treatments. Yet the high prices of some drugs have left government health programs strapped, or forced them to limit coverage. For example, one promising hepatitis C treatment is so expensive that some state Medicaid programs have chosen to cover its cost for only the sickest patients.

"Triage, triage, triage," said Emily Scott, a Tennessee factory worker with hepatitis C who was denied coverage for the new treatment. "They set their price so high that we poor folks can't afford it."

Despite such cases, four researchers from Precision Health Economics warned in an article last month that any government controls on drug prices could actually shorten the average American's life by two years by discouraging development of new drugs.

"As the pace of innovation slows, future generations of older Americans will have lower life expectancy relative to the status quo," they wrote. The article, funded by the pharmaceutical trade group PhRMA, was published in Forum for Health Economics & Policy, of which Goldman is the editor-in-chief and co-founder. More than half of the editors listed on its masthead are current or former consultants at the firm.

Just after Precision Health Economics co-founder Dana Goldman completed his Ph.D. in economics at Stanford, in 1994, he was diagnosed with type 1 diabetes. He was 29 years old. With a pump he wears every day, he takes insulin to treat the disease.

"I would pay hundreds of thousands of dollars if I could take one pill that would make me better," Goldman said.

His desire for a cure led to a new scholarly interest: the economics of medical innovation. Because there were few government funders for research in the field, he turned to industry. In 2005, Goldman established the firm with Lakdawalla and Philipson.

The headquarters of Precision Health Economics sits in a West Los Angeles office building flanked by palm trees, about 10 miles from Goldman's academic center at USC. Goldman's assistant at USC is also an executive assistant at the consulting firm. Daniel Shapiro, director of research compliance at USC, said that both Goldman and Lakdawalla were in compliance with the university's standards on consulting.

Precision Health Economics has counted at least 25 pharmaceutical and biotech companies and trade groups as clients. The roster includes Abbott Nutrition, AbbVie, Amgen, Biogen, Bristol-Myers Squibb, Celgene, Gilead, Intuitive Surgical, Janssen, Merck, the National Pharmaceutical Council, Novartis, Otsuka, Pfizer, PhRMA, rEVO Biologics, Shire and Takeda. The firm has 85 staff members in nine locations.

Over the years, the founders recruited an impressive cadre of high-profile academics to consult for these clients. Early in 2016, the firm boasted more than two dozen academic advisers and consultants from top universities on its website. (The site later stopped identifying professors by their university affiliations.) The list of associates has also included some policy heavyweights who recently left the government, including a top official from the Congressional Budget Office, a senior economist from the White House's Council of Economic Advisors, and an FDA commissioner. About 75 percent of publications by the firm's employees in the past three years have either been funded by the pharmaceutical industry or have been done in collaboration with drug companies, a ProPublica review found.

Some academics worry that a tight relationship with industry might suggest bias. "I personally find, when your enterprise relies so substantially on a particular source of funds, you will tend to favor that source," said Princeton economist Uwe Reinhardt.

Goldman says his industry connection has helped him ask better questions.

"The right way to do these things is not to push away the private sector, but to engage them," he told ProPublica. "If we end up with a world where everyone who has a voice in a debate must be free of perceived bias, we lose the importance of the diversity of ideas." In a later interview, he added, "You have to separate the appearance of the bias with actual bias."

These ideas were recently echoed in an op-ed that he wrote with Lakdawalla in the online publication The Conversation.

"To be sure, collaboration with industry supplements our income through consulting fees. But no matter who funds our research—foundations, government, or companies—we apply the same template to our work," wrote Goldman and Lakdawalla. "The ivory tower is not always the best place to understand the social benefits of treatments, the incentives for medical innovation, and how aligning prices with value can aid consumers."

Engaging the private sector has indeed boosted Goldman's income. According to federal conflict of interest forms filed last year, when he served on an advisory panel to the Congressional Budget Office, Goldman earned consulting income from the firm in the range of $25,000 to $200,000, on top of his income as a USC professor. He also has more than $500,000 in equity in the firm. Precision's Harley says Goldman and Lakdawalla each have equity stakes of less than 1 percent, indicating that the firm is worth at least $50 million. Lakdawalla and Philipson have not publicly disclosed their consulting incomes.

In April 2015, Precision Health Economics was acquired by a privately held biotech company, Precision for Value. Terms weren't disclosed.

Precision Health Economics raised its profile in 2013 when the president's annual economic report cited a cancer study by several of the firm's principals and consultants. To some critics, though, the study showed how industry funding can taint academic research.

Originally published in Health Affairs, where Goldman also serves on the editorial board, the study found that Americans paid more for cancer care than Europeans but had better survival gains.

As the study acknowledged, it was funded by Bristol-Myers Squibb, a company that at the time was developing a much-anticipated cancer treatment. It was priced at more than $150,000 per year when it eventually came on the market. All three founders of Precision Health Economics were listed as authors of the Health Affairs article, alongside one of their employees, yet none of the founders disclosed their ties to their consulting firm in the published study. In an interview, Goldman said this might have been an "oversight."

Goldman later emailed ProPublica to clarify that the journal was aware that the study was a Precision Health Economics publication and that Goldman and his co-founders were affiliated with the firm. Goldman has published more than 25 articles and letters to the editor in Health Affairs since co-founding Precision Health Economics, and only five have listed the connection.

"This affiliation is clearly not a secret and I include it where relevant," Goldman wrote in the email. "The bottom line is that disclosure policies vary across journals, journal editors, and over time. Definitions of what is 'relevant' are also subject to their own judgments."

Donald Metz, executive editor of Health Affairs, said the journal followed its policy of leaving disclosure to the "authors' discretion." Its editorial staff did not exclude any information on conflicts or affiliations that the authors provided alongside their draft, he said.

As the cancer study gained national recognition, its methodology and findings came under fire. Researchers from Dartmouth College tried and failed to reproduce the results. Cancer care in the U.S., their research found, may actually provide less value than cancer care in Europe, considering cost.

"We know that [the U.S. health care system] is more disorganized and disorganization is more expensive, so it's surprising to believe that the U.S. would perform better in a cost-effectiveness sense," said Samir Soneji, one of the authors of the counter-study and an assistant professor of health policy at Dartmouth. The science in the original study, Soneji says, was "questionable."

Soneji was not alone in his criticism. Aaron Carroll, a pediatrics professor at the Indiana University School of Medicine, reviewed the methodology and concluded that the Precision Health Economics researchers had used a measure that can frequently be misinterpreted. Instead of relying on mortality rates, which factor in a patient's age of death, the study employed survival rates, looking at how long people live after diagnosis. Cancer screening, which can increase survival rates, is more frequent for some cancers in the U.S. than in other countries, Carroll says.

"When they wrote that paper using survival rates, they were clearly cherry picking," Carroll told ProPublica. "If the arguments are flawed and people keep using them, I would be concerned that they have some other motive."

The founders of Precision Health Economics defended their use of survival rates in a published response to the Dartmouth study, writing that they "welcome robust scientific debate that moves forward our understanding of the world" but that the research by their critics had "moved the debate backward."

Precision Health Economics has become a prominent booster of a new way of setting drug prices—based on their overall value to society. Value is determined by comparing the drugs' cost with their effectiveness in saving lives and preventing future health expenses.

Pharmaceutical companies have traditionally justified their prices by citing the cost of research and development, but recent research on drug pricing has challenged this argument. Many of the largest drug companies spend more on sales and marketing than on developing their drugs. And notably, one researcher has found that about 75 percent of new molecular entities, which are considered the most innovative drugs, trace their initial research funding back to the government.

"There is substantial evidence that the sources of transformative drug innovation arise from publicly funded research in government and academic labs," said Dr. Aaron Kesselheim, an associate professor at Harvard Medical School whose research looks at the cost of pharmaceuticals. Pharmaceutical pricing, he says, is primarily based on what the market can bear.

Many early proponents of value pricing, including American health insurers, saw it as a way to rein in drug prices. Some nations, particularly those with national health systems, like the U.K., rely on official cost-effectiveness analyses to decide which drugs to pay for. Overpriced drugs are sometimes denied coverage. This powerful negotiating tool has helped keep drug prices down abroad.

Efforts to establish similar practices in the U.S., however, have been stymied by lobbying from patient groups, many of them funded by the pharmaceutical industry, contending that value pricing could lead to rationing of health care. More recently, though, the industry has used academic consultants to help it redefine the concept of "value" to justify its pricing.

At the congressional briefing on the new hepatitis C drugs, Harvard Medical School associate professor Anupam Jena, a Precision Health Economics consultant, suggested that part of a drug's value is earning enough profit that pharmaceutical companies are enticed to develop treatments for other diseases. Otherwise, Jena said, "you don't incentivize innovations that actually deliver value, and so the next cure … may not be developed."

Princeton's Reinhardt said pricing drugs based on this notion of value could give the industry carte blanche to charge whatever it wants. "If you did value pricing and say it's OK for the drug companies to charge up to what the patient values his or her life to be, you are basically saying that the pharmaceutical companies can take your savings," he said. "American society will not stand for that."

Not long after the controversy over its cancer research, Precision Health Economics became embroiled in another academic spat related to a client's product. This time, it was over a breakthrough treatment that, injected one to two times per month, could help millions of Americans with high cholesterol. At the $14,000-per-year price set by one of its makers, Amgen, the PCSK9 inhibitor could also hike the nation's annual prescription drug costs by an unprecedented $125 billion, or 38 percent. Its price in the U.S. is twice as much as in the U.K.

The U.S. price of the drug has come under vigorous attack from the nonprofit Institute for Clinical and Economic Review. ICER, which began as a small research project at Harvard Medical School, studies the cost-effectiveness of drugs, balancing their value to patients against the impact of their cost on society. The Centers for Medicare and Medicaid Services proposed a new rule in March 2016 that includes the use of value-based pricing studies, specifically citing the work of ICER.

The industry has attacked many of the institute's studies, particularly those that find a treatment is overpriced. Some patient groups have contended that ICER emphasizes cost savings because it receives funding from health insurers. However, foundations are ICER's biggest source of funding, and it is also supported by the pharmaceutical industry and government grants. The pharmaceutical lobby has similarly attacked the Drug Effectiveness Review Project, a coalition of state Medicaid agencies and other payers, accusing it of using its studies to justify "rationing."

ICER concluded in 2015 that the new cholesterol treatment, the PCSK9 inhibitor, should cost about one-fifth what Amgen is charging. A few months later, Philipson, the Precision Health Economics co-founder, and Jena wrote an op-ed in Forbes, citing the institute's research and deriding its approach to value pricing as "pseudo-science and voodoo economics." Only Philipson disclosed his ties to Precision Health Economics, and neither academic disclosed that Amgen was a client of the firm.

After being asked by ProPublica about the lack of transparency, Forbes added a disclosure statement to the op-ed. "Manufacturers of PCSK-9 inhibitors and novel treatments for hepatitis C, such as Amgen, Gilead, and Abbvie, are clients of Mr. Philipson's consulting firm, Precision Health Economics, for which Dr. Jena also works," the publication noted. "In general, the pharmaceutical and biotechnology companies which retain Precision Health Economics benefit from higher drug prices."

Goldman, along with Precision Health Economics employees and two Harvard professors, including Jena, published their own study on the cholesterol drug in the American Journal of Managed Care, where Goldman serves on the editorial board. They found that the new cholesterol drugs were indeed cost-effective at the listed prices. The article disclosed the authors' ties to Precision Health Economics and the source of funding: Amgen.

The drug is "not cheap, but it's a good deal" for patients who need it, Goldman said, after his team's economic models calculated its net value between $3.4 trillion and $5.1 trillion over 20 years.

ICER's finding that the PCSK9 inhibitor was overpriced was later affirmed in a related study published in the peer-reviewed Journal of the American Medical Association, or JAMA. Associates of Precision Health Economics again rushed to Amgen's defense. Philipson and an Amgen executive wrote a letter to the editor of JAMA to dispute the study's conclusion that the price should be about $4,500 per month, less than a third of the drug's average price.

The two studies made different assumptions that shaped their conclusions. Dr. Dhruv Kazi, one of the authors of the JAMA study and an associate professor at the University of California San Francisco, said that the Precision Health Economics study assumed that there were fewer eligible patients who would take the drug, lowering the cost to society. It also posited that they had a higher risk of cardiac events, like heart attacks, boosting the drug's value as measured in lives saved.

"This is an example where you would end up assuming that the population is at higher risk than is true for the real world population and that would make your drug look better," Kazi said. "It's not a wild idea to think that a cost-effectiveness study funded by industry would look more favorable" to the industry's viewpoint, he said. "If that weren't the case, they wouldn't fund it."

Jena said the patient population for the Precision Health Economics study more accurately reflected the real world. One should not automatically assert that a study is "invalid or flawed" because of industry funding, he added.

The JAMA study "over-exaggerated the cost" of the drug and "unnecessarily rang 'alarm bells,'" said Amgen spokeswoman Kristen Neese.

Amgen has ties to all three founders of Precision Health Economics. Working for other firms, Philipson has twice testified

GDUFA

The US Food and Drug Administration (FDA) approved more generic drugs in 2015 than ever before and is on track to meet all of its goals from the *Generic Drug User Fee Act of 2012* (GDUFA) by 2017, according to the first annual report from FDA's Office of Generic Drugs (OGD).

More than 700 generic drugs were approved and tentatively approved in 2015, which was the highest figure ever; and in December, FDA granted the highest number of approvals and tentative approvals in a single month (99) since the generic drug program began, according to the new report, which echoed FDA's performance report to Congress from late March.

The approvals are an important way in which FDA is able to keep the cost of drugs in check, particularly as generic drugs now account for 88% of prescriptions dispensed in the US, and they have saved the US health system $1.68 trillion from 2005 to 2014.

The success of OGD is thanks in a large part to GDUFA, under which industry agreed to pay approximately $300 million in fees each year of the five-year program, which is set to end in 2017. Negotiations for the next GDUFA agreement between FDA and industry are ongoing and will focus particularly on FDA's performance goals.

"Generic Drug Approvals Hit New Record in 2015, FDA Report Shows," by Zachary Brennan, Regulatory Affairs Professionals Society, April 13, 2016.

as an expert witness for Amgen, defending the company's rights to drug patents, according to his curriculum vitae. The other two founders, Goldman and Lakdawalla, are principals at the Leonard D. Schaeffer Center for Health Policy and Economics at USC, which received $500,000 in late 2016 from Amgen for an "innovation initiative," according to public disclosures. Goldman said the funds were unrestricted and could be used at the center's discretion. Robert Bradway, the CEO and chair of Amgen, is on the advisory board of the university center, and Leonard Schaeffer, a professor at USC and the namesake of the center, sat on Amgen's board of directors for nearly a decade.

With funding from Amgen, the Schaeffer Center hosted a forum in Washington, D.C., in October 2015 on the affordability of specialty drugs. Before a panel focused on the new cholesterol treatment, Goldman cautioned against lowering drug prices.

"We know that the pricing of these treatments is often controversial," he told the crowd of policymakers, which included Sen. Bill Cassidy, R-La., a physician who sits on the Health, Education, Labor and Pensions Committee. "If we dropped all the prices today, in the long run, we wouldn't have any innovation."

The PCSK9 inhibitor's price inhibits access for some patients who need it. Scott Annese, a 50-year-old computer technician from South Daytona, Florida, has diabetes and a total blood cholesterol level topping 260. After he suffered a heart attack and had two stents inserted in his left coronary artery, his doctor prescribed a statin, a low-cost drug to lower cholesterol. However, the statin combined with his diabetes to cause painful side effects, including muscle aches, cramping, and soreness in his legs that incapacitated him, he said. Amgen's drug, his doctor told him, was the only other option.

But Annese, who makes $13.50 an hour, couldn't afford the new drug. He doesn't have health coverage through his job and says Obamacare, especially with its rising premiums, is too expensive for him. He tried to get insurance through Medicaid, but he earns too much to qualify. His last option, he said, is Amgen's patient assistance program, which he has applied for. His application is pending. "If you're in the industry to help people, you're not helping them if you raise the drugs to the point that they can't afford it," said Annese. "The drug companies are hurting the people who need it most."

Gilead Sciences' $84,000 list price for its highly effective treatment for the hepatitis C virus prompted dozens of state Medicaid programs and prison systems to restrict treatment to only the sickest patients. A congressional investigation in 2015 found that Gilead, which purchased the drug from a smaller pharmaceutical company, had set the price of the treatment at the peak it thought the market could bear, more than double what the drug's original developers had suggested.

"Gilead pursued a calculated scheme for pricing and marketing its hepatitis C drug based on one primary goal, maximizing revenue, regardless of the human consequences," said Sen. Ron Wyden, D-Ore., when he presented the findings of the congressional investigation.

While Precision Health Economics often portrays itself as an advocate for wider access to vital medications such as the hepatitis C drugs, the high price of those drugs forces some payers, such as the Medicaid programs, to ration them. As a result, the professors may influence who ultimately gets the drug and who doesn't. The impact is reverberating in the rugged hills of eastern Tennessee, where hepatitis C is spreading due to the opioid epidemic. Because the virus can be asymptomatic for years, only a fraction of those infected know they are carriers, leading many to spread the potentially fatal liver disease unknowingly, mostly by sharing needles.

> "*Pharmaceutical patent rights that run for too long or that are defined too expansively will deprive people of drugs because purchasers, including governments, cannot afford them.*"

Patent Laws Keep Drug Prices High

Matthew Rimmer

In the following viewpoint, Matthew Rimmer argues that governments should control the practice known as "evergreening," wherin pharmaceutical patents are prolonged, delaying the opportunity for generic equivalents of those drugs to be manufactured and made available to the public. Evergreening allows drug companies to make more money while consumers are stuck paying high prices. Rimmer is a professor of intellectual property and innovation law at Australia's Queensland University of Technology. He has published widely on patent law and access to medicines.

As you read, consider the following questions:

1. How does evergreening work?
2. Why did the Pharmaceutical Patents Review propose a conservative approach to granting patent rights?
3. What are the estimated savings from the proposed reduction in patent length?

O n the 20th March 2014, the Australian Government published the final version of an independent policy report, the *Pharmaceutical Patents Review Report*, after much public pressure.[1] The report has significant implications in respect of patent law, pharmaceutical drugs, the Pharmaceutical Benefits Scheme, and trade policy—particularly in respect of the Trans-Pacific Partnership. The independent report has also highlighted the opportunity of great savings for the Australian health-care system through shortening patent term extensions. The economist Peter Martin has warned: "Australia's enthusiastic approach to extending the life of pharmaceutical patents has cost the economy 'billions of dollars' an independent review has found."[2]

This paper provides a short review of the Pharmaceutical Patents Review Report, and highlights key recommendations. In particular, it looks at the call by the review for a frugal, parsimonious approach to the granting of patent rights in respect of pharmaceutical drugs in Australia. The paper considers the recommendations of the Pharmaceutical Patents Review Report to shorten and reduce patent term extensions. It examines the proposed recommendations to address the problem of evergreening. This paper also considers the debate over data protection. Finally, the Pharmaceutical Patents Review Report is critical of Australia's passive approach to the negotiation of intellectual property and international trade. The findings of the report emphasize the need for Australia to protect its public health interests in the negotiation of the Trans-Pacific Partnership.

The Pharmaceutical Patents Review Report

Under the leadership of Julia Gillard, the Australian Labor Party took a keen interest in the impact of patent law upon research, patient care, and the provision of health-care.[3] Indeed, Gillard had taken a particular interest in patent owners engaging in the nefarious practice of "evergreening"—extending the life of patents beyond their natural term by making minor changes.

The report had been commissioned by Mark Dreyfus QC MP, a Parliamentary Secretary for Innovation in the former Australian Labor Party Government. The review was designed to examine whether Australia's patent system was "effective in securing timely access to competitively priced pharmaceuticals and in supporting innovation and employment in the industry." The report was undertaken by three well-respected experts—Tony Harris; intellectual property academic Professor Dianne Nicol, and economist Dr Nicholas Gruen.

Initially, the Minister for Industry Ian McFarlane for the new Coalition Government was reluctant to release the final report. Melissa Parke MP—the member for Fremantle—asked in the Australian Parliament: "By what date will he release the final report of the 2012 Pharmaceutical Patents Review, and is he considering the draft recommendations released in April 2013?."[4] Ian McFarlane responded that "the Government has no plans to release the final report at this stage" and "the Government is not considering the recommendations made by the panel in the draft report." Ian McFarlane maintained: "As the Pharmaceutical Patents Review was commissioned by the previous government and conducted by an independent panel, the government is not obliged to release the report."

Dr Deborah Gleeson from LaTrobe University highlighted the failure of the Coalition Government to publish the report.[5] She noted: "While Treasurer Joe Hockey is complaining that Australia is running out of money to fund the health system, the Coalition Government has buried a report with recommendations for large-scale savings on drug costs." But the burial of the final report, the submissions made to the review and the economic estimates of the costs of patent term extension is particularly concerning in the light of the current Government's search for cost-cutting measures. Gleeson lamented: "It will be a shame if we end up with knee-jerk policies like $6 GP co-payments in an attempt to cut health system costs when sensible reforms to patent law could generate hundreds of millions of dollars of savings through the

Pharmaceutical Benefits Scheme." She warned that "an even worse prospect would be the further extension of patent monopolies through our international trade agreements, adding hundreds more millions to the health budget."

Information activist Brendan Molloy—a member of Pirate Party Australia, and Electronic Frontiers Australia—sought to reveal the report through freedom of information requests.[6]

In the end, the Australian Government relented, and published the Pharmaceutical Patents Review Report. The Australian Government was non-committal about the recommendations of the report:

> Government statement on the Pharmaceutical Patent Review final report. The Pharmaceutical Patent Review was commissioned by the previous government and conducted by an independent panel. The review panel provided its final report to the previous government in May 2013, which did not release the report. The government notes that the report is one of a number of reviews of the pharmaceutical system conducted during the term of the previous government. The government has no plans to respond to the report at this stage but may take information in the report into account when considering future policy. The views expressed and recommendations made in the report are those of the review panel and do not necessarily reflect government policy.

It is a credit to the Minister Ian MacFarlane to release the report, so that there could be a full and frank public discussion in respect of patent law and pharmaceutical drugs.

A Frugal Approach to Patent Rights

The final 233-page report—Pharmaceutical Patents Review Report—is essential reading for those interested in intellectual property and public health. The combination of Tony Harris, Dianne Nicol, and Nicholas Gruen has ensured that the work is a multi-disciplinary investigation into patent law and pharmaceutical drugs. The report is a thorough, systematic, and balanced piece of work. The report is informed wide-ranging consultations and interactions with industry, government, academia, and consumers.

The Pharmaceutical Patents Review Report emphasizes that "the question of how much patent protection to offer is crucial." The study noted:

> Pharmaceutical patent rights that run for too long or that are defined too expansively will deprive people of drugs because purchasers, including Governments, cannot afford them. They can also constrain follow on innovation: too weak a patent system means patients will suffer because the industry has inadequate incentives to develop new drugs.

The Pharmaceutical Patents Review proposed a frugal approach to the grant of patent rights. The Review recommended that 'the Government should expeditiously seek a situation where Australia has strong yet parsimonious IP rights—that is, rights that are strongly enforced and that provide the incentive necessary to underpin an appropriate level of investment in innovation—but that are not defined so broadly as to impose costs on innovation or other activity without commensurate benefits." The report suggested: "Australia should take a leadership role in seeking consensus with jurisdictions with similar interests to identify and pursue a range of changes in international patent law and practice along these lines." The report observed: "While the patent system must be strong to be effective, it should also be parsimonious, avoiding restrictions on trade and innovation that are not necessary for it to deliver incentives to innovate."

Patent Term Extensions

The Pharmaceutical Patents Review Report makes a number of important recommendations relating to patent term extensions. Under Australia law, the patent term lasts for twenty years. Since 1998, pharmaceutical drug patents can obtain additional term extensions for up to a further years. The inquiry noted:

An important part of the terms of reference of this inquiry is to evaluate the extension of term (EOT) that the Australian patent system allows. It applies to some pharmaceuticals for which patentees have taken at least five years from the effective patent filing date to obtain regulatory approval for the pharmaceutical's use. The current scheme dates from 1998. It aims to attract investment in pharmaceutical R&D in Australia, as well as providing an effective patent term forpharmaceuticals more in line with that available to other technologies. The scheme currently provides an effective patent term of up to 15 years.

The report noted that patent term extensions were expensive for the Australian Government: "The estimate for 2012–13 is around $240 million in the medium term and, in today's dollars, around $480 million in the longer term." The report stressed: "The total cost of the EOT to Australia is actually about 20 per cent more than this, because the PBS [Pharmaceutical Benefits Scheme] is only one source of revenue for the industry." The report emphasized: "Using the patent scheme to preferentially support one industry is inconsistent with the TRIPS rationale that patent schemes be technologically neutral."

The inquiry canvassed a number of policy options to address patent term extensions:

Australia is required by AUSFTA to provide some form of pharmaceutical EOT but its scope and length are not specified. Actual savings obtained from reducing the term of the extension would be affected by many factors, including price changes caused by increasing sales volumes, the 16 per cent mandated price reduction following the entry of a second drug, the influence of competing generic manufacturers and reductions from price disclosure mechanisms. But there are timing issues in reducing the EOT provisions immediately without compensation. Savings from the options considered in this report, including the recommendation to reduce the effective life of extended Australian pharmaceutical patents, would take several years to reach full effect.

The inquiry recommended: "The Government should change the current EOT to reduce the maximum effective patent life provided from 15 years." There was a difference of opinion between the members of the review: "Harris and Gruen support reducing the effective life to 10 years, whereas Nicol supports reducing the effective life to 12 years." The report advised: "The length of the extension should be calculated as being equal the number of days between the patent date and the date of first inclusion on the Australian Register of Therapeutic Goods minus 20 years less the maximum effect patent life." The report noted: "The current 5 year cap on extensions should remain, providing a maximum of 25 years patent term for extended patents."

The Pharmaceutical Patents Review Report emphasized that there could be significant savings to Australian tax-payers from the reform of Australian patent term extensions. The recommendation by Harris and Gruen was predicted to provide for massive savings:

> Mr Harris and Dr Gruen recommend reducing the effective patent life from 15 to 10 years. Over time this would save the PBS approximately $200 million a year. in today's dollars, based on current pricing arrangements (that the entry of generics will lead to price falls of 35 per cent) which the Government has agreed with Medicines Australia. The savings would grow in line with PBS costs which are growing at 4.5% per annum, substantially faster than real GDP. If the Government secured all of the pricing benefits allowed by the entry of generics, annual savings in today's dollars could amount to around $400 million which would similarly be expected to grow with PBS costs. This is calculated on data that generics have led to a 70% price reduction in the United States. This is consistent with recent findings by the Grattan Institute that the price of generics paid by the PBS is several times the price secured by relevant Australasian Governments.

It is calculated that Professor Nicol's recommendation to shorten the effective patent life would result in significant savings: "The estimated savings resulting from this reduction would be approximately $130 million a year." Moreover, it was noted: "If a 70% price reduction from generic entry was achieved as discussed above, the savings would be approximately $260 million a year."

Patent Standards and the Problem of Evergreening

The former High Court of Australia Justice Michael Kirby observed in a case that patent law "should avoid creating fail-safe opportunities for unwarranted extensions of monopoly protection that are not clearly sustained by law."

The Pharmaceutical Patents Review Report also addressed the pernicious problem of evergreeening—where patent owners seek to indirectly extend the life of patent protection, beyond its natural monopoly. The report noted:

> In most developed countries, including the United States and Europe, there are concerns about pharmaceutical manufacturers using patents and other management approaches to obtain advantages that impose large costs on the general community. The cost arises because these actions impede the entry of generic drugs to the market. Although some find the term to be a pejorative, relevant literature has dubbed such actions "evergreening": steps taken to maintain the market place of a drug whose patent is about to expire.

The report noted: "It is probable that less than rigorous patent standards have in the past helped evergreening through the grant of follow-on patents that are not sufficiently inventive." The report called for improvements in the oversight of patent quality standards: "The Panel sees a need for an external body, the Patent Oversight Committee, to audit the patent grant processes to help ensure these new standards are achieved, and to monitor whether they inhibit the patenting of follow-on pharmaceuticals which promote evergreening with no material therapeutic benefit."

Data Protection

The inquiry also considered the vexed question of data protection for pharmaceutical drugs. The report noted:

> When an originator seeks regulatory approval for a drug, it must provide data to the TGA[Therapeutic Goods Administration] demonstrating the drug's safety and efficacy. Although these data remain confidential to the TGA, it may use them after a five year period to approve a generic or equivalent drug. This saves the pointless replication of tests to show safety and efficacy.

The pharmaceutical drugs industry argued that the five-year period of data exclusivity in Australia was too short. The Pharmaceutical Patents Review Report found that there was no need to extend data protection in respect of pharmaceutical drugs:

It is conceivable that drugs might not be brought to Australia, for example, because regulatory and marketing costs cannot be recouped within five years. Medicines Australia submits that some of its members chose not to supply a total of 13 drugs to the Australian market because of the inadequacy of the data exclusivity period. However, they are only able to identify three of these, and the Panel's analysis—shown in chapter 8—suggests they are not convincing. AbbVie offers a more compelling example, but even there the Panel believes that expanding data exclusivity for all or for a wide class of drugs is a poorly targeted response to issues affecting a small number of pharmaceuticals. A policy of subsidising drug development discussed above seems more appropriate.

The report noted: "The Government should actively contribute to the development of an internationally coordinated and harmonised system where data protection is provided in exchange for the publication of clinical trial data."

Such a finding has a broader significance, given the push by the United States for stronger data protection in the Trans-Pacific Partnership.

Trade and the Trans-Pacific Partnership

The Pharmaceutical Patents Review Report observed that "Larger developed countries that are major net IP exporters have tended to seek longer and stronger patents, not always to the global good." The report warned: "The acquiescence of Australia and other countries to that agenda means that some features of Australia's patent law are of little or no benefit to patentees but impose significant costs on users of patented technologies."

The Pharmaceutical Patents Review Report was highly critical of Australia's passivity in international negotiations over intellectual property and trade. The report found:

> In their negotiation of international agreements, Australian Governments have lacked strategic intent, been too passive in their IP negotiations, and given insufficient attention to domestic IP interests. For example, preventing MFE [Manufacturing for Export] appears to have deprived the Australian economy of billions of dollars of export revenue from Australian based generic manufactures. Yet allowing this to occur would have generated negligible costs for Australian patentees. The Government does not appear to have a positive agenda regarding the IP chapters of the TPP Agreement.

The report noted: "The Government has rightly agreed to only include IP provisions in bilateral and regional trade agreements where economic analysis has demonstrated net benefits, however this policy does not appear to be being followed."

The Pharmaceutical Patents Review Report recommended that "the Government should ensure that future trade negotiations are based on a sound and strategic economic understanding of the costs and benefits to Australia and the world and of the impacts of current and proposed IP provisions, both for Australia and other parties to the negotiations." The Pharmaceutical Patents Review Report stressed that "the Government should strongly resist changes—such as retrospective extensions of IP rights—which are likely to reduce world economic and social welfare and it should lead other countries in opposing such measures as a matter of principle."

Furthermore, the Pharmaceutical Patents Review Report recommended: "Given the current constraints placed on Australia by its international obligations, as an interim measure the Government should actively seek the cooperation of the owners of Australian pharmaceutical patents to voluntarily agree to enter into non-assertion covenants with manufacturers of generic pharmaceuticals seeking to manufacture patented drugs for export." In its view, "This would help them avoid the embarrassment of Australia's trade and investment performance being penalised by its previous agreement to strengthen IP rights."

The Pharmaceutical Patents Review Report warned: "There are signs that these past failures are being replicated in the current Trans-Pacific Partnership (TPP) negotiations because small, net importers of intellectual property, including Australia, have not developed a reform agenda for the patent system that reflects their own economic interests and those of the world."

WikiLeaks has published a draft text of the Intellectual Property Chapter of the Trans-Pacific Partnership.[7] The Intellectual Property Chapter contains a number of measures, which support the position of pharmaceutical drug companies and the biotechnology industry.[8] Notably, the United States has pushed for extensions of the patent term in respect of pharmaceutical drugs, including where there have been regulatory delays. There has been a concern that the Trans-Pacific Partnership will impose lower thresholds for patent standards, and result in a proliferation of evergreening. There has also been a concern about patent-registration linking to marketing regimes. The United States has also pushed for the protection of undisclosed data for regulatory purposes. There has been wide concern that the Trans-Pacific Partnership will result in skyrocketing costs for health-care systems in the Pacific Rim.

Disturbingly, Australia has been quite passive in the debate over intellectual property and public health in the Trans-Pacific Partnership negotiations. Other countries—such as Canada, New Zealand, and Malaysia—have argued, more passionately, that there is a need for the patent system to protect public health.

Moreover, the Trans-Pacific Partnership also contains an investment chapter, with investor-state dispute settlement. The brand name pharmaceutical drug company Eli Lilly have deployed an investor clause under the North American Free Trade Agreement to challenge Canada's drug patent laws. There is a concern that the investor-state dispute settlement regime in the Trans-Pacific Partnership could be deployed to challenge public health measures, and reforms to the patent system designed to combat problems such as evergreening.

Professor Joseph Stiglitz has been concerned about the impact of the Trans-Pacific Partnership upon equality and human rights.[9] He observed that "Agreements like the TPP have contributed in important ways to this inequality." Stiglitz warned: "Corporations may profit, and it is even possible, though far from assured, that gross domestic product as conventionally measured will increase." He feared that "the well-being of ordinary citizens is likely to take a hit." The Nobel Laureate warned that "Trickle-down economics is a myth." Stiglitz concluded that "enriching corporations—aas the TPP would—will not necessarily help those in the middle, let alone those at the bottom."

Conclusion

The Pharmaceutical Patents Review Report is a landmark report, which should receive serious consideration by policy-makers in Australia, and throughout the Pacific Rim. The study deserves a wide readership amongst intellectual property academics, economists, and health experts. The Pharmaceutical Patents Review Report provides a cautionary warning of the need to design a patent regime, which is appropriate and well-adapted to Australia's economy, research and development system, and public health-care regime:

The report also highlights the problem of patent owners seeking corporate welfare in domestic patent law reform and international negotiations. There is a need to guard the integrity of the patent system against being co-opted by brand-name pharmaceutical companies and biotechnology companies. Patent term extensions and evergreening undermine the public bargain of patent law to promote the progress of science and the useful arts. There is a need to ensure that the public domain is not captured by private companies. The report should be a guide in Australia's future approach to domestic patent law reform, and international negotiations over intellectual property and trade. The study highlights the need for greater consideration of the economic impact of legal revisions—particularly in the area of patent law and pharmaceutical drugs. Australia's patent regime should protect the public health of its citizens.

Notes

1. Tony Harris, Dianne Nicol, and Nicholas Gruen, Pharmaceutical Patents Review Report, Canberra, 2013, http://www.ipaustralia.gov.au/pdfs/2013-05-27_PPR_Final_ Report.pdf

2. Peter Martin, "Drug Patents Costing Billions," The Sydney Morning Herald, 2 April 2013,http://www.smh.com.au/national/health/drug-patents-costing-us-billions-20130402-2h52i.html

3. Matthew Rimmer, 'Julia Gillard, Big Pharma, Patent Law, and Public Health', The Conversation, 27 November 2012, https://theconversation.edu.au/julia-gillard-big-pharma-patent-law-and-public-health-10226

4. Melissa Parke MP, "Pharmaceutical Patents Review," House of Representatives, Australian Parliament, 11 February 2014, http://parlinfo.aph.gov.au/parlInfo/search/display/display.w3p;query=Id%3A%22chamber%2Fhansardr%2F55d46158-f865-4a9f-9015-36543a3b6b7b%2F0183%22

5. Deborah Gleeson, "Cost-Cutting Crusade Ignores Health Savings," ABC, The Drum, 6 March 2014, http://www.abc.net.au/news/2014-02-28/gleeson-cost-cutting-crusade-ignores-vital-health-report/5289726

6. Brendan Molloy, "Pharmaceutical Patents Review" Right to Know, 28 February 2014, https://www.righttoknow.org.au/request/pharmaceutical_patents_review_fi

7. WikiLeaks, "Advanced Intellectual Property Chapter for All 12 Nations with Negotiating Positions (30 August 2013 consolidated bracketed negotiating text)," https://wikileaks.org/tpp/

8. Alexandra Phelan and Matthew Rimmer, "Trans-Pacific Partnership #TPP #TPPA Drafts Reveal a Surgical Strike against Public Health," East Asia Forum, 2 December 2013,http://www.eastasiaforum.org/2013/12/02/tpp-draft-reveals-surgical-strike-on-public-health/

9. Joseph Stiglitz, "On the Wrong Side of Globalization," The New York Times, 15 March 2014,http://opinionator.blogs.nytimes.com/2014/03/15/on-the-wrong-side-of-globalization/

> "*The length of US market exclusivity is one of the reasons why so many companies want to introduce their treatments in the US first (and why new drugs generally reach the market in the US more quickly than elsewhere).*"

Market Exclusivity Delays the Availability of Cheaper Generic Drugs

Zachary Brennan

In the following viewpoint, Zachary Brennan examines the reasons why it takes so long for generic drugs to come to market. Many Americans depend on the affordablility of generic drugs and are hit hard when such generics are not available. They are told that the FDA is to blame for delays in generics coming to market because of backlogs of abbreviated new drug applications (known as ANDAs). However, Brennan argues that the real reason for such delays has to do with the fact that there is a patent and market exclusivity system that rewards pharmaceutical companies even after they've recouped the money that it took for research and development. Brennan is managing editor for RAPSorg's regulatory focus.

"Patents vs. Market Exclusivity: Why Does it Take so Long to Bring Generics to Market?" by Zachary Brennan, Regulatory Affairs Professionals Society, August 17, 2016. Zachary Brennan, Managing Editor, Regulatory Focus, RAPS. Reprinted by permission.

As you read, consider the following questions:

1. Why does a drug have patents that do not expire until eight years after a generic could potentially come to market?
2. How many years of exclusivity do orphan drugs receive?
3. How many years of exclusivity do new chemical entities (NCEs) receive?

I t's well known that generic drugs are just as safe and effective as their brand name counterparts. They're the cheap knockoffs that help more people around the world gain access to innovative and sometimes life-saving treatments; the boring copycats made by companies you've never heard of and sold in plain bottles with little fanfare.

But what most people, particularly those outside the pharmaceutical industry, don't realize is that what's constraining the dissemination of these small molecule generics, particularly in the US (where the prices of brand name drugs continue to rise), isn't the US Food and Drug Administration (FDA) and the backlog of abbreviated new drug applications (ANDAs) (as Congress has complained), but a patent and market exclusivity system that can reward pharmaceutical companies long after they've recouped their research and development (R&D) expenses and, at times, hefty profits (Gilead's hepatitis C treatments have brought in more than $40 billion over the past few years, the vast majority of which is in US sales).

And though it's easy to point a finger at the US and blame the pharmaceutical companies' lawyers for creating such a system and at times gaming it (e.g. pay-for-delay deals), the length of US market exclusivity is one of the reasons why so many companies want to introduce their treatments in the US first (and why new drugs generally reach the market in the US more quickly than elsewhere).

Jacob Sherkow, an associate professor in intellectual property law at New York Law School, explained to *Focus:* "The strength of the US pharma patent system is one of the reasons why a lot of companies do their main research and development here in the US. The thing driving them to sell their products in the US first is we're one of the few (if not only) industrialized countries that doesn't have a nationalized health system … A drug that's a flop in the US will not make up that lost revenue elsewhere."

Patents but no Market Exclusivity?

And what's even less well known outside the pharmaceutical industry is that there are major differences between a pharmaceutical company having a patent for a brand name drug and having the market exclusivity to keep competing generics from gaining a share of the brand name drug's sales.

As FDA explains: "Patents and exclusivity work in a similar fashion but are distinctly different from one another. Patents are granted by the patent and trademark office anywhere along the development lifeline of a drug and can encompass a wide range of claims. Exclusivity is exclusive marketing rights granted by the FDA upon approval of a drug and can run concurrently with a patent or not. Exclusivity is a statutory provision and is granted to an NDA [new drug application] applicant if statutory requirements are met. [See 21 C.F.R. 314.108.] Exclusivity was designed to promote a balance between new drug innovation and generic drug competition."

Take, for example, AstraZeneca's diabetes treatment Bydureon (exenatide) and its patents and term of exclusivity as provided by FDA's Orange Book (the Bible of pharmaceutical patent information). AstraZeneca has 18 patents covering the product, two of which don't expire until 2026. However, the product's market exclusivity expires in September 2018, which begs the question: Why does a drug have patents that do not expire until eight years after a generic could potentially come to market?

Sherkow explains that this example is actually a typical case, noting: "Short answer here: this is the way generic entry is structured. For ANDAs to be approved, they need to certify that

THE PROBLEM WITH PATENTS

The U.S. could rein in rising drug prices by being more selective about giving patents to pharmaceutical companies for marginal developments, a study concludes.

That's because brand-name drugs with patents that grant exclusivity account for about 72 percent of drug spending, even though they are only about 10 percent of all prescriptions dispensed, according to the study, published Tuesday in *JAMA*, the journal of the American Medical Association.

"You've got a bunch of different tactics that are being used that can extend that exclusivity," says Aaron Kesselheim, a professor at Harvard Medical School and the study's lead author.

He says the patent office is too permissive in granting patents for drug properties that have no bearing on its therapeutic value.

Under the current law, new chemically based medications approved by the Food and Drug Administration get the right to sell their drugs with no competition from generics for five to seven years. More complex biologic drugs get 12 years of protection.

But drugmakers can also use their patents to keep competitors out of the market.

The study found that new drugs have a median 12.5 years of exclusive market access, and it's even longer for completely new medications.

Kesselheim says drugmakers often use "life-cycle management" tactics to extend their exclusive market access.

He pointed to a cholesterol drug named Tricor-1 as an example. The medication was made by Abbott Labs. When a company applied to make a generic version, Abbott sued, delaying the competitor's entry to the market, according to an account excerpted in the blog The Incidental Economist.

As the lawsuit proceeded, Abbott changed the dosage of the drug, named it Tricor-2, and aggressively moved patients to the new version. When the generic version of Tricor-1 was finally approved, very few people were taking it anymore.

Kesselheim says the patent office is charged with protecting inventions that are "novel, useful and non-obvious," but that it has been lax in interpreting those parameters. If patents were harder to get on nonessential properties of medications, there would likely be more competition sooner.

"We did a study a while back and found one HIV medication has over 100 different patents covering formulations and crystal structures and methods of use," he says.

"Tighter Patent Rules Could Help Lower Drug Prices, Study Shows," by Alison Kodjak, npr, August 23, 2016.

they don't infringe any patents listed in the Orange Book ... which is one of the reasons they'll add these patents to discourage generic companies from filing ANDAs in the first place," particularly because of the expense of the litigation.

Elaine Blais, head of the litigation department at Goodwin Procter's Boston office, also told *Focus* that under Hatch-Waxman, which is the Act outlining the process by which an ANDA can be filed, an ANDA is often subject to an automatic 30-month stay of approval when a brand name drug company files a patent infringement suit.

"In theory, the 30-month stay allows the brand and generic to litigate patent issues to determine whether the patent will block competition (is it valid and infringed?) after the regulatory exclusivity expires," she says.

Other differences between patents and market exclusivity include: Patents expire 20 years from the date of filing, while exclusivity is granted on the basis of the type of drug. For instance, orphan drugs (treatments for rare diseases affecting fewer than 200,000 people in the US) get seven years of exclusivity, while new chemical entities (NCEs) get five years. Companies can also get other types of exclusivity if certain statutory criteria are met, though those generally don't last for longer than three years.

And when pediatric exclusivity is granted to a drug, FDA says a period of 6 months of exclusivity is added to all existing patents and exclusivity on all applications held by the sponsor for that active moiety.

Another major difference: Patents can be expired before drug approval, issued after drug approval and anywhere in between, according to FDA, while exclusivity is granted upon approval.

"Some drugs have both patent and exclusivity protection while others have just one or none. Patents and exclusivity may or may not run concurrently and may or may not encompass the same claims. Exclusivity is not added to the patent life. Expired patents and exclusivity are not included in the published list," FDA adds.

And though FDA makes clear the distinctions between patents and exclusivity, Sherkow told us that he cannot recall there ever being a case where a generic company got to tell FDA, "there are literally no patents covering this reference listed drug."

International Markets

Outside the US, where exclusivity is generally shorter and governments can negotiate drug prices, pharmaceutical companies often reap less profits over a shorter period of time.

But in some countries, like India and Brazil, they have what are known as compulsory licenses, which basically allow local companies to produce and locally market drugs that haven't reached a point in time when generic competition is legally allowed.

The Pharmaceutical Research and Manufacturers of America (PhRMA) argues that compulsory licenses should only be issued in "exceptional situations," such as when there is a pressing public health need, though other groups, like Doctors Without Borders, have explicitly called for the use of compulsory licenses in places like India to bring down drug prices.

Sherkow told us he thinks compulsory licenses aren't so much a problem of the licenses themselves but a fear of the unknown.

"You can't underestimate the fear that a lot of IP counsel have in terms of what patent breaking means for their company's risks at large," he said. "It may be 'irrational' for companies to throw away an R&D program because there might be a compulsory license scheme, but that might actually drive the decision making ... we see this in physician malpractice tort claims."

And though the behavior might not be rational, it's that fear that drives the decision making, he said, adding, "We shouldn't pretend that that's not changing the calculus for what companies look into for R&D and that's bad."

> *"Much of the debate on the cost of medicines focuses on the initial U.S. price. But prices vary within different sectors of U.S. health care, across nations, and over time."*

Drug Prices Are High for Legitimate Reasons

Michael Rosenblatt, MD

In the following viewpoint, Michael Rosenblatt provides a different perspective on the reasons why prescription drug costs are as high as they are in the United States. A big part of Rosenblatt's argument is that the cost is often the most popular topic of a prescription drug, when in reality, the priority should be its health-improving and life-saving benefits. Rosenblatt also explains that consumers' perception of price has changed, and a lot of that has to do with the fact that more people than ever are paying for out of pocket medical expenses. Rosenblatt is the chief medical officer of Flagship Pioneering. He previously served as the chief medical officer of Merck and the dean of the Tufts University School of Medicine.

"The Real Cost of "High-Priced" Drugs," by Michael Rosenblatt, Harvard Business School Publishing, November 17, 2014. Reprinted by permission.

As you read, consider the following questions:

1. Generics make up what percentage of prescriptions in the US today?
2. How long after market introduction do patents expire for most new drugs?
3. By 2050, how much will the US expenditure be toward Alzheimer's disease?

Much of the recent press about drug pricing has taken a narrow view of the topic. As the chief medical officer of a global pharmaceutical company, I view patients' access to medicines as an issue of such importance that it demands a broader perspective. I also see the matter from two other vantage points: as a physician who has cared for patients and as an academic who led a Boston teaching hospital and medical school. With these complementary perspectives, I assess the value of a medicine not in isolation, but as part of an interlocking system with the patient at its center. Consider these key principles and policies related to pricing:

1. The Average Price Over Time

Much of the debate on the cost of medicines focuses on the initial U.S. price. But prices vary within different sectors of U.S. health care, across nations, and over time. And for most new drugs, patents expire approximately 12 years after market introduction. In the U.S. today, generics make up 86% of prescriptions.

Consider atorvastatin (Lipitor), a leading cholesterol-lowering statin, whose initial cost of more than $5 a tablet fell by 95% — to 31 cents a tablet — when the drug went generic. The osteoporosis drug alendronate (Fosamax) used to cost $2.60 per day; now it is 28 cents. Such drugs continue to be used widely at low prices that will persist indefinitely.

So what is the true cost of a medicine: the initial price or the average price over the course of decades? No other health care expense (hospital charges, physician fees, and so on) undergoes so dramatic a decline in price. Given the prices after patents expire, innovative drugs essentially become ongoing "gifts" to society.

2. The Value of Long-Term Benefits

Focusing only on the cost of a medicine—without considering its health-improving or life-saving benefits, or consequent reductions in other health care expenses—ignores its real value. While the cost is immediate, the benefits often don't accrue for years. I co-led a team that brought alendronate from the laboratory to worldwide use. The incidence of osteoporosis-related hip fractures in women declined by 40% since the mid-1990s, when alendronate and (subsequently) similar drugs were introduced in the United States. Preventing such fractures avoids suffering for individuals and saves thousands of lives. It also lowers the costs of caring for people who would otherwise have endured a fracture.

Improving patients' adherence to their medication regimens does increase spending on drugs, but the long-term savings can be so compelling that, for example, some insurers now offer all diabetes medicines to their members with no copay. The nonpartisan Congressional Budget Office acknowledges that use of prescription drugs can reduce health care spending.

Nevertheless, recognizing value is difficult in the U.S. because patients switch insurers relatively frequently. Long-term benefits, such as fewer heart attacks or fractures, take time to accrue, so the health plan that initially spends on the medicine often doesn't reap the financial benefit. However, it may accrue the benefit of another insurer's spending when it acquires a new patient.

3. Changes in Patients' Perceptions of Price

Out-of-pocket expenses for medicines are growing. The old drug-copay arrangements, often a flat $10 to $30, shielded patients (but not their insurers) from knowing the full price. With higher copays and deductibles, patients often think prices are rising much faster than they actually are. Many patients now pay $2,500 to $3,000 of their health care costs before insurance coverage kicks in. The result: Some patients pay more today for a generic drug than they paid for the original patented drug, even though the actual cost has declined dramatically.

4. The New Benefits of Competition

Competition among research-driven companies brings better medicines to patients, but it also has become so intense that, for the first time, blockbuster drugs are rapidly becoming obsolete. The breakthrough hepatitis C therapy, telaprevir (Incevik), was withdrawn from the market only four years after approval, when sofosbuvir (Sovaldi) became available. Competitive market forces have helped Medicare Part D achieve substantial savings: 2013 spending was 50% below projections ($50 billion versus $99 billion).

In the context of these new realities, we need creative and practical solutions on multiple fronts:

A. Pricing That Promotes Much-Needed Invention

"Innovation" is an overused term. Most health care innovations, such as standardized surgical protocols or antimicrobial stewardship, are *refinements* that improve efficiency while enhancing quality of care. Medicines and vaccines, in contrast, are necessary *inventions*. Consider the economic burden of Alzheimer's disease: The current U.S. annual expenditure of $200 billion will balloon to $1.2 trillion (in current dollars) by 2050. Does anyone seriously believe that more efficient hospital, nursing home, and home care will avert the crisis? I can imagine only one solution: new drugs that arrest, delay, or prevent Alzheimer's. Yet only 7% of Alzheimer-drug trials are NIH-funded, despite a failure rate of 99% among the 400+ clinical trials of 33 agents in the past decade. What company will gamble on agent #34 without adequate incentives?

B. Pricing That Sustains a Proven Business Model

Very few organizations can undertake the arduous, risky, expensive process of drug R&D. There is a common misconception that NIH research is responsible for most drug breakthroughs. In reality, the pharmaceutical industry's investment in R&D (more than $50 billion in 2012) far exceeds the NIH's total budget (about $30 billion in 2012). NIH-funded basic research is foundational. However, although the NIH work sometimes generates drug "leads," industry's enormous investment is what translates those basic advances into actual treatments for patients.

Explaining the investment and persistence needed for successful R&D is challenging. The path is long, not linear, and littered with failures. Only 20% of approved medicines generate revenues that exceed average R&D investment. Consider this comparison: In 2013, Apple spent $4.5 billion on R&D, or 2.6% of net sales. Merck spent nearly twice that amount, $7.5 billion, representing 17% of net sales. Furthermore, it takes about five times longer (10 to 15 years) to develop a medicine than a smartphone.

When I first joined the pharmaceutical industry, regulatory approval was the "finish line" for R&D. Now drugs must be tested in clinical trials in multiple geographic locations. Large outcome trials, post-approval monitoring, and comparative-effectiveness studies have become routine. Such ongoing investment, added to R&D costs, helps explain why companies committed to research cannot compete with generics on price. Unless an appropriate return on investment is possible, biopharmaceutical companies will be unable to undertake the risky long-term R&D that addresses unmet medical needs and can yield overall cost savings.

C. Pricing That Takes a Global View

Drug prices in the U.S., where the private market is less highly regulated, are typically higher for innovative drugs than in other developed countries (though the U.S. government mandates substantial discounts for Medicaid patients and other needy populations). U.S. prices are substantially lower for generic drugs. In many other countries, health authorities set prices below market levels using criteria unrelated to the value of the drug to patients and society. As a result, the U.S. shoulders a substantial portion of the cost of inventing new medicines. Pricing that reflects the true value of medicines across all developed countries would enhance the flow of inventions that meet important unmet medical needs worldwide.

D. Continued Corporate Responsibility

Companies like Merck continue to offer assistance programs to U.S. patients who cannot afford certain medicines. We also consider a country's level of economic development and public health needs when establishing our prices. When market-based solutions are not available, companies like Merck also often donate medicines, especially in low-income regions of the world. I have seen firsthand the benefits of international programs that help address and prevent HIV/AIDS, hepatitis B infection, and neglected tropical diseases such as river blindness. A sustainable business model that drives innovation bolsters our ability to make such philanthropic efforts.

What the Future Holds

Even a perfect solution to today's pricing issues is unlikely to address all the challenges ahead. We're entering an era of personalized or precision medicine. For certain diseases, we will identify subgroups of patients who respond better than others to a drug or experience fewer side effects. These targeted drugs will have higher value. But the cost of developing a drug for 10,000 people is similar to that of developing one for 1 million people. Without changes in drug development, regulation, or both, it will be difficult to price medications in ways that recover investment for many specialized therapies.

Nonetheless, if we can support invention, we will certainly save lives and money.

Periodical and Internet Sources Bibliography

The following articles have been selected to supplement the diverse views presented in this chapter.

Ricardo Alonso-Zaldivar, "Did landmark laws from Congress enable high drug prices?" U.S. News, Sept. 29, 2016. https://www.usnews.com/news/business/articles/2016-09-29/did-landmark-laws-from-congress-enable-high-drug-prices.

Peter Bach, "Why Drugs Cost So Much," The New York Times, Jan. 14, 2015. https://www.nytimes.com/2015/01/15/opinion/why-drugs-cost-so-much.html.

Susan Jaffe, "USA grapples with high drug costs," The Lancet, Nov. 28, 2015. http://www.thelancet.com/journals/lancet/article/PIIS0140-6736(15)01098-3/fulltext.

Sarah Kliff, "EpiPen's 400 Percent Price Hike Tells Us A Lot About What's Wrong With American Health Care," Vox, August 23, 2016. https://www.vox.com/2016/8/23/12608316/epipen-price-mylan.

Nadia Kounand, "Why pharmaceuticals are cheaper abroad," CNN, Sept. 28, 2015. http://www.cnn.com/2015/09/28/health/us-pays-more-for-drugs/index.html.

Sydney Lupkin, "FDA Fees On Industry Haven't Fixed Delays In Generic Drug Approvals," npr, September 1, 2016. http://www.npr.org/sections/health-shots/2016/09/01/492235796/fda-fees-on-industry-havent-fixed-delays-in-generic-drug-approvals.

Laurie McGinley, "Cancer drug prices are so high that doctors will test cutting doses," The Washington Post, June 8, 2017. https://www.washingtonpost.com/news/to-your-health/wp/2017/06/08/how-these-cancer-doctors-plan-to-reduce-patients-drug-costs-without-touching-prices/?utm_term=.6c3f0119a186.

Jayne O'Donnell and Deirdre Shesgreen, "Cancer patient, outraged by sky-high drug prices, organizes others to fight them," USA Today, Feb. 22, 2017. https://www.usatoday.com/story/news/politics/2017/02/22/new-patient-group-focuses-drug-prices-amid-bipartisan-concern/98168146/.

Jeanne Whalen, "Why the U.S. Pays More Than Other Countries for Drugs," The Wall Street Journal, Dec. 1, 2015. https://www.wsj.com/articles/why-the-u-s-pays-more-than-other-countries-for-drugs-1448939481.

Nancy Yu, Zachary Helms, and Peter Bach, "R&D Costs For Pharmaceutical Companies Do Not Explain Elevated US Drug Prices," Health Affairs, Mar 7, 2017. http://healthaffairs.org/blog/2017/03/07/rd-costs-for-pharmaceutical-companies-do-not-explain-elevated-us-drug-prices.

OPPOSING
VIEWPOINTS®
SERIES

CHAPTER 2

Why Don't Insurance Companies Cover All Prescription Drugs?

Chapter Preface

Having a high level understanding of why prescription drugs are so expensive in the United States helps provide a foundation for the next step in understanding the debates surrounding big pharma and drug prices. It's time to dig deeper into another important question surrounding the pharmacy and health care industries: Why do prescription companies cover the costs for certain drugs but then neglect others? This is a question that continues to baffle consumers who depend on certain drugs to live, and as you can probably guess, it all comes down to the bottom line.

As readers will learn after they read through the viewpoints offered in chapter 2, there are a few main reasons why insurance companies cover some drugs and not others, and it all boils down to money and revenue. If an insurance company like CVS Caremark or Express Scripts cannot negotiate a discount with a drug manufacturer, they will drop that medication from their coverage list, thus forcing consumers to pay out of pocket for it, which can be extremely pricey.

Another driving force behind insurance coverage on prescription medications has a lot to do with the US government and its lack of action being taken on inflating drug prices. While most other countries have national health programs with government entities who either negotiate the price of the drug or actually set the cost themselves and the coverage that will accompany it, the United States does not. What that does is allow the drug manufacturers to set the price themselves, and with the added wrinkle that these manufacturers are also given exclusive rights for many years to certain medications, it makes it even more difficult for insurance companies to cover these costly medications, which in turn means consumers are left to take on the high costs themselves.

This chapter will provide readers with more of a full-picture understanding of the pharmaceutical and health care landscape, as they will now see the connection—and disconnection—between prescription drug manufacturers and insurance companies. The viewpoints in chapter 2 provide the reader with context in preparation for the next chapter, which discusses the ethics of charging high prices for medications.

> *"Countries with national health programs have government entities that either negotiate drug prices or decide not to cover drugs whose prices they deem excessive. No similar negotiating happens in the U.S."*

Government-Protected Monopolies Drive Drug Prices Higher

Sydney Lupkin

In the following viewpoint, Sydney Lupkin argues that government-protected monopolies are the reason why consumers are paying high costs for prescription drugs. Lupkin points out that this process is unique to the US only, as other countries with national health programs have government entities that negotiate or decide on the cost and coverage of prescription medications. She states that the drug companies have essentially created a monopoly on the industry, and they're setting their own rules, regulations, and prices. Lupkin goes on to shed light on the fact that drug makers are given exclusive rights to certain medications, which only compounds the issue. Lupkin is a journalist who covers drug prices and specializes in data reporting for the Kaiser Health News enterprise team.

"Government-Protected 'Monopolies' Drive Drug Prices Higher, Study Says," by Sydney Lupkin, Kaiser Health News, August 23, 2016.

As you read, consider the following questions:

1. Which program must cover all drugs approved by the Food and Drug Administration, regardless of whether a cheaper, equally or more effective drug is available?
2. What percentage do drug prices decline to of their original brand name cost once there are two generics on the market?
3. Pharmacists in how many states are required by law to get patient consent before switching to a generic drug?

The "most important factor" that drives prescription drug prices higher in the United States than anywhere else in the world is the existence of government-protected "monopoly" rights for drug manufacturers, researchers at Harvard Medical School report today.

The researchers reviewed thousands of studies published from January 2005 through July 2016 in an attempt to simplify and explain what has caused America's drug price crisis and how to solve it. They found that the problem has deep and complicated roots and published their findings in JAMA, the journal of the American Medical Association. The study was funded by the Laura and John Arnold Foundation with additional support provided by the Engelberg Foundation.

"I continue to be impressed at what a complex and nuanced problem it is and how there are no easy solutions either," said lead study author Dr. Aaron Kesselheim, a professor who runs the Program on Regulation, Therapeutics and Law at Harvard Medical School and Brigham and Women's Hospital. "As I was writing, the enormity of the problem continued to shine through."

Five key findings in the JAMA review:

1. Drug manufacturers in the U.S. set their own prices, and that's not the norm elsewhere in the world.

Countries with national health programs have government entities that either negotiate drug prices or decide not to cover drugs whose prices they deem excessive. No similar negotiating happens in the U.S.

When a Republican-majority Congress created the Medicare drug benefit in 2003, they barred the program that now covers 40 million Americans from negotiating drug prices. Medicaid, on the other hand, must cover all drugs approved by the Food and Drug Administration, regardless of whether a cheaper, equally or more effective drug is available. And private insurers rarely negotiate prices because the third party pharmacy benefits managers that administer prescription drugs, such as Express Scripts and CVS Health, often receive payments from drug companies to shift market share in their favor, according to the study.

2. We allow "government-protected monopolies" for certain drugs, preventing generics from coming to market to reduce prices.

In an effort to promote innovation, the U.S. has a patent system that allows drug manufacturers to remain the sole manufacturer of drugs they've patented for 20 years or more. The FDA also gives drug manufacturers exclusivity for certain products, including those that treat people with rare diseases.

But sometimes, drug companies deploy questionable strategies to maintain their monopolies, the study says. The tactics vary, but they include slightly tweaking the nontherapeutic parts of drugs, such as pill coatings, to game the patent system and paying large "pay for delay" settlements to generics manufacturers who sue them over these patents.

And this is a serious problem, the study concludes, because drug prices decline to 55 percent of their original brand name cost once there are two generics on the market and to 33 percent of original cost with five generics.

3. The FDA takes a long time to approve generic drugs.

Application backlogs at the FDA have led to delays of three or four years before generic manufacturers can win approval to make drugs not protected by patents, the study says.

4. Sometimes, state laws and other "well-intentioned" federal policies limit generics' abilities to keep costs down.

Pharmacists in 26 states are required by law to get patient consent before switching to a generic drug, the authors wrote. This reportedly cost Medicaid $19.8 million dollars in 2006 for just one drug: a statin called simvastatin whose brand name is Zocor. Costs ran higher because pharmacists didn't get patient consent and Medicaid had to pay for the costlier brand name drug even though a cheaper product was available.

5. Drug prices aren't really justified by R&D.

Although drug manufacturers often cite research and development costs when defending high prescription prices, the connection isn't exactly true, Kesselheim and his team found, citing several studies. Most of the time, scientific research that leads to new drugs is funded by the National Institutes of Health via federal grants. If not, it's often funded by venture capital. For example, sofosbuvir, a drug that treats hepatitis C, was acquired by Gilead after the original research occurred in academic labs.

"Arguments in defense of maintaining high drug prices to protect the strength of the drug industry misstate its vulnerability," the authors wrote, adding that companies only spend 10 percent to 20 percent of their revenue on research and development. "The biotechnology and pharmaceutical sectors have for years been among the very best-performing sectors in the U.S. economy."

Instead, the price tags are based on what the market will bear, they wrote.

In general, fixing America's drug price problems won't be easy, the study authors concluded. Congressional gridlock and the power of the pharmaceutical lobby make allowing Medicare to negotiate Part D prices an unlikely possibility. And leaving that aside, policymakers must find a way to tighten rules and strengthen oversight surrounding patent protections and exclusivity without chilling innovation, Kesselheim said.

Those not involved in the study said the fact that it was published in JAMA is meaningful because the authors are able to speak directly to doctors.

"I think the most significant thing about this is not necessarily what he's saying but who he's saying it to," said Kenneth Kaitin, who directs the Tufts Center for the Study of Drug Development. "In part, the concern over rising drug prices is something that physicians have been more aware of lately...They've still been for the most part on the sidelines of these issues."

Kaitin said the exception has been the American Society of Clinical Oncology and the physicians at Memorial Sloan Kettering Cancer Center.

Dr. Joshua Sharfstein, the Associate Dean for Public Health Practice and Training at the Johns Hopkins Bloomberg School of Public Health, said Kesselheim's study provides a "bird's eye view" of how the U.S. became an outlier when it comes to drug prices, without getting lost in the weeds.

"It also illustrates that there is not a single policy that is going to address the range of challenges that our health system faces around drug pricing," Sharfstein said.

> *"The managers of pharmacy benefits pit brand-name drugs that treat the same condition against each other, rather than waiting for generic drugs to come on the market and drive prices down."*

Consumers Are Caught in the Middle When the Interests of Drug Companies and Insurers Conflict

Alison Kodjak

In the following viewpoint, Alison Kodjak enlightens those who depend on their prescription medications for continued good health and survival that some medications may no longer be covered by prescription insurance companies. Two of the largest, CVS Caremark and Express Scripts released their 2017 list of approved drugs, with more medications than ever appearing on the excluded medications list, including drugs used to treat cancer, diabetes, hepatitis, and asthma. Kodjak argues that the motive behind not covering certain drugs is tied to big savings for the insurance companies, which they in turn try to pass off as savings for their customers. Kodjak is a health policy correspondent on NPR's Science Desk.

"Will Your Prescription Meds Be Covered Next Year? Better Check!" by Alison Kodjak, npr, August 15, 2016. Reprinted by permission.

As you read, consider the following questions:

1. How many drugs did CVS Caremark list on its "we won't pay" list?
2. How much does CVS says its formulary management will save its customers over the next five years?
3. How many people does Express Scripts cover?

The battle continues to rage between drug companies that are trying to make as much money as possible and insurers trying to drive down drug prices. And consumers are squarely in the middle.

That's because, increasingly, prescription insurers are threatening to kick drugs off their lists of approved medications if the manufacturers won't give them big discounts.

CVS Caremark and Express Scripts, the biggest prescription insurers, released their 2017 lists of approved drugs this month, and each also has long lists of excluded medications. Some of the drugs newly excluded are prescribed to treat diabetes and hepatitis. The CVS list also excludes some cancer drugs, along with Proventil and Ventolin, commonly prescribed brands of asthma inhalers, while Express Scripts has dropped Orencia, a drug for rheumatoid arthritis.

Such exclusions can take customers by surprise, says Lisa Gill, an editor at *Consumer Reports'* "Best Buy Drugs."

"We've talked to dozens and dozens of people who find themselves at the pharmacy counter, shocked to find out that the drug is no longer covered," she tells Shots. Patients can appeal the decision in individual cases, but that process can be arduous.

CVS Caremark has been the more aggressive of the two prescription insurers, listing roughly 130 drugs on its "we won't pay" list. Express Scripts lists 85 and has a policy of not banning cancer drugs or mental health medications.

The threat of kicking drugs off their covered lists — which are known as formularies — is a powerful way to drive discounts, says

Adam Fein, CEO of the Drug Channels Institute and author of a blog on prescription drug markets.

"Exclusions are one reason why discounts have been growing," he tells Shots.

Express Scripts and CVS Caremark only started actively using their lists this way in 2012. Both firms claim they've already extracted huge savings for *their* customers: the health insurance companies and private corporations who hire them to manage their prescription drug plans.

CVS says its formulary management will save its customers $9 Billion over the next five years.

For 2017, the company has excluded nine drugs that it deems "hyper-inflationary" — defined as "products with egregious cost inflation that have readily available, clinically appropriate and more cost-effective alternatives," says Carolyn Castel, a spokeswoman for CVS Caremark.

The company specifically looks at drugs whose prices more than triple over three years, Castel says.

Those drugs include three skin creams that combine an over-the-counter ingredient, such as hydrocortisone or aloe, with a generic prescription drug to make a new and expensive brand name medication.

CVS manages prescription coverage for about 75 million people. For the first time in 2017 it is dropping from its list two so-called biologic drugs — the diabetes drug Lantus and Neupogen, a medicine commonly given to patients undergoing chemotherapy to help boost white blood cells and immunity. Instead, the company will pay for alternatives known as biosimilars. It was an important move; because of the way these drugs are made, biosimilars aren't exact equivalents of the medications they replace.

But that's part of the strategy of formulary exclusions. The managers of pharmacy benefits pit brand-name drugs that treat the same condition against each other, rather than waiting for generic drugs to come on the market and drive prices down.

Explaining Formularies, Generics, and Preferred Drugs

A formulary is a list of medications that your insurance company will help you pay for. This list is reviewed and changed by the insurance company every few months.

The drugs in a formulary are often listed in 2 or more groups, depending on how much of the cost you are expected to pay. The amount you're expected to pay is called your co-pay. When a drug company develops a new drug, it gives it a brand name. Brand names are the names you usually see in ads on TV and in magazines–names like Claritin and Advil.

For several years after the drug is developed, laws prevent other drug companies from copying it. When other companies start manufacturing and selling the drug, their versions are usually known by a different name–the generic name. This is often the chemical name. For instance, the generic name of Claritin is loratadine and the generic name of Advil is ibuprofen.

Generic drugs are chemically the same as brand-name drugs, and they are often less expensive. That's why many insurance plans encourage you to use generic drugs.

Often 2 brand-name drugs help treat the same problem. Your insurance company may be able to get one less expensively than the other. That drug becomes a preferred drug, and the other becomes non-preferred. That's usually why you pay more for non-preferred drugs.

Sometimes an insurance company will move a drug from the preferred list to the non-preferred list. If this happens to you, your doctor might be able to prescribe a preferred drug that would cost you less money and work just as well for you.

"Prescriptions and Insurance Plans," American Academy of Family Physicians, February 2012.

Express Scripts covers about 85 million people, according to a recent investor presentation. Spokesman David Whitrap says the company tried to avoid excluding drugs; he recognizes the exclusions are an inconvenience to patients.

"Express Scripts will only ask members to switch their medication if there is a clinically equivalent alternative," he tells

Shots, "and only if that switch delivers a significant cost savings for their employer."

For patients, the inconvenience can be minor, or it can be a real medical issue.

"From a consumer standpoint, you can wind up with a much bigger headache, with a lot more time invested in trying to sort out your prescriptions," says Gill.

That's because when the excluded medications don't have generic alternatives that pharmacists can substitute automatically, patients have to go back to their doctor to get a prescription for a new drug.

"It's a tricky trade-off," says Jack Hoadley, a professor and researcher at Georgetown University's Institute for Health Policy. "Am I getting enough of a discount to offset the inconvenience?"

Sometimes the drug on the approved list doesn't work as well for some patients as the one that's been kicked off.

"You end up having to switch to a drug that your prescriber thinks is less than optimal for treating your particular health condition," Hoadley says.

"We believe that employers have the greatest potential to influence some of those actors and, ultimately, to chip away at high drug prices."

Employers Should Use Their Power to Cut Drug Prices

Robert Galvin, MD, and Roger Longman

In the following viewpoint, Robert Galvin and Roger Longman consider that company employers actually have the power to lower the cost of prescription drugs. The authors argue that employers have more power, clout, and experience with insurance companies, and that as seasoned buyers, they should know how to negotiate prices down with suppliers, insurance companies, and pharmacy benefit managers (PBMs). While the authors do present the option of single-payer systems, they ultimately come to the conclusion that this option wouldn't work in the US because it is perceived as too close to socialism. Galvin is the CEO of Equity Healthcare, a health management company owned by the Blackstone Group; an operating partner at Blackstone; and a member of the Institute of Medicine. Longman is the CEO of Real Endpoints, a health care analytics company that focuses on pharmaceutical reimbursement.

"Who Has the Power to Cut Drug Prices? Employers," by Robert Galvin, MD and Roger Longman, Harvard Business School Publishing, December 1, 2015. Reprinted by permission.

As you read, consider the following questions:

1. What pricing program allows hospitals to buy drugs at 30% to 50% of the retail price but then bill at full price for patients with insurance?
2. Single-payer systems are most popular in what countries?
3. What are pharmacy benefit managers (PBMs) hired to do?

Why do medications cost so much, particularly specialty drugs that treat the most serious conditions? Mostly because U.S. drug companies can price them however they want. Some of their justifications are reasonable—for instance, high prices fund research. Others, like the notion that drug treatment lowers total medical costs, are far from proven.

But pharmaceutical companies don't deserve all of the blame for high drug prices. Lots of other actors in purchasing, distribution, and brokerage have greater incentives to keep prices high than to lower prices or choose drugs that reduce longer-term medical and business costs, like absenteeism.

We believe that employers have the greatest potential to influence some of those actors and, ultimately, to chip away at high drug prices. To appreciate the power that employers have in this area, you must first understand how competing incentives work in the world of drug pricing.

Competing Incentives

Hospitals, for example, can take advantage of the 340B pricing program, which allows them to buy drugs at 30% to 50% of the retail price but then bill at full price for patients with insurance. And even organizations that, theoretically, are paid to help hold down drug costs sometimes have incentives to do the opposite. Take insurers and pharmacy benefit managers (PBMs), which are hired to manage drug costs for employer-based health plans.

Indeed, it's smart for employers like GE, IBM, and Google to contract with these specialist entities and have them decide

Pharmacy Benefit Managers

Pharmacy benefit managers, or PBMs, are companies that process prescriptions for insurance companies and corporations, and use their size to negotiate low prices with drug makers and pharmacies. They act as an intermediary between the payor and everyone else in the healthcare system.

One major PBM, Express Scripts, is dramatically decreasing its coverage for some bulk ingredients of compounded drugs. They're citing high prices, and arguing that "by and large, compounded medications do not provide any additional clinical value over what is currently available." The company will block coverage for approximately 1,000 active ingredients.

Three other PBMs—Optum Rx (part of the insurance company United Health Group), CVS Caremark, and Catamaran—have placed restrictions on compounded drug ingredients. Harvard Pilgrim Health Care, the largest insurer in New England, ended coverage for compounded drugs altogether except for children and medically necessary drugs for adults.

Note the language these PBMs are using: "They don't provide any additional clinical value." "Only medically necessary drugs." Why in the world are insurers—or worse, their drug purchasing managers—determining what is "medically necessary" rather than one's personal physician? Pharmaceutical companies and insurance companies are negotiating prices and profits between themselves, without a single thought to the best interests of patients. And, as we have noted before, attacking compounded medications gives more of a monopoly to FDA-approved drugs.

Recently enacted legislation already restricts access to compounded drugs—though everything will hinge on what finally ends up on the "FDA-approved" list—and the new limits on interstate commerce for traditional pharmacies have already driven up compounding costs. With access to compounded medication being restricted by government regulation, and with insurance company PBMs cutting coverage, demand for compounded bulk ingredients will naturally decrease and prices will almost certainly rise further. This greatly threatens the existence of the small compounding pharmacies for whom we advocate.

A new coalition of patients, patient advocacy groups, pharmacists, physicians, pharmacies, and healthcare organizations has arisen to fight these changes. Patients and Physicians for Rx Access is seeking to raise awareness about access to compounded medications. They explain just how important compounding is to American healthcare— and how safe the medications really are.

"Insurance Company Drug Managers Now Deciding What's Medically 'Necessary'," by Alliance for Natural Health USA, Alliance for Natural Health USA, August 5, 2014.

which drug among several competitors their employees should get first, at what cost, and which medical policies should govern the use of that drug. After all, insurers and PBMs can spread the costs for research, negotiation, and decision making about drug-reimbursement policies across all of their clients.

However, PBMs and insurers may have business objectives that differ from those of their clients. For one, they're not always at risk for the cost of drugs—the clients are. Also, a PBM or a pharmacy department of an insurer gets a substantial portion of its drug-related profit from rebates. These are payments negotiated with manufacturers that return, via the PBM or payer intermediary, a percentage of the drug's price to the payer—for example, to an employer that contracts with a PBM or an insurer.

Here's a simplified version of how these rebates work:

To get the business, the PBM or plan typically guarantees a minimum rebate on every prescription, say $60. On a $300 script, that's a 20% net reduction in the cost to the employer (final price: $240). As an incentive for the PBM or plan to negotiate even harder—maybe get a 30% rebate (in this case, another $30)—it often takes home 30% to 50% of anything above the guaranteed rebate. In this example, if the split were 50/50, the employer would pay $225, net, for the prescription and the PBM would get $15. Not a bad deal.

In the old days—maybe five years ago, when most prescriptions ranged from $200 to $400—rebates worked to the employer's advantage. But for a specialty drug, costing say $50,000, a rebate of 20% means that the employer pays a net $40,000 and the PBM pockets $10,000 (plus other fees for processing and, sometimes, for handling the prescription through a specialty pharmacy division). Meanwhile, the $60 guarantee becomes meaningless.

Now let's assume *both* a smaller rebate (10%) and a lower price ($25,000) for the same drug. The $60 rebate is still meaningless, but now the net cost to the employer is $22,500 (much better than $40,000) and the PBM's profit is just $2,500. If you're the PBM, do you want the manufacturer to price the drug at $50,000 or $25,000?

It's also true that very large employers sometimes get virtually the whole rebate, not a 50/50 split. But don't cry for the plans and PBMs, which know how to tack on various fees, often including a specialty pharmacy fee of about 2%. That cost covers the overhead and profit margin of a necessary part of the distribution system. But 2% on a $500 drug is $10; on a $50,000 drug, it's $1,000. Again, a higher drug price means a more profitable supply chain.

(Insurance companies would argue, by the way, that they shouldn't be lumped in completely with PBMs, because most insurers manage their pass-through and full-risk businesses with the same pharmacy policies. For the full-risk business, insurers care about drug prices, at least to the extent that they can't just raise premiums for employers.)

Options for Lowering Prices

The easiest way to lower drug prices would be with a single-payer system, which most European countries have. That payer would be on the hook for all medical costs and would therefore have the incentives—and the clout—to negotiate lower prices. But we can't envision that happening in the U.S., where some political players would cry "socialism." So we're left looking to employers and the Centers for Medicare and Medicaid Services (CMS), which runs Medicare.

Changing CMS reimbursement practices is a Sisyphean task, given the congressional and lobbyist opponents. Even a relatively small proposal last year—narrowing the "protected classes" rules that, in essence, require reimbursement for all drugs in six therapeutic areas—was shot down decisively by drug companies, patient advocacy groups, and legislators.

Employers' weak-kneed behavior is more baffling—no other group has a greater stake in buying smarter. But employers have always been reluctant actors in the health care system, as they feel out of their depth. Some companies, like Honeywell and Nielsen, have taken tough steps to control costs, with no loss in employee satisfaction. But don't count on a sea change in employer buying behavior—when push comes to shove, they can always shift costs to their employees.

What Employers Can Do

Employers must recognize that, like it or not, the buck stops with them. Patients can hardly negotiate for themselves, but employers can be much more aggressive in getting PBMs and payers to have skin in the drug-pricing game.

Our sense is that PBMs, at least, are willing to listen. Express Scripts, for example, recently proposed capping its customers' total exposure to the PCSK9-inhibitor class of cholesterol-lowering drugs. If their customers spend more than a pre-set amount, Express Scripts eats the overage. Certainly, Express wouldn't do this without a clear idea of how much its clients would be spending. Notably, those clients must agree to follow Express's rules about who gets the expensive drugs—and must use Express's specialty pharmacy. But it's a very good start.

We certainly don't expect employers to start writing drug-coverage policies and doing their own contracting. But, as seasoned buyers, they know how to negotiate with suppliers, such as insurers and PBMs—and they should not be afraid to do it. It's now easier to understand the tradeoffs among competitive drugs, thanks to tools like the Institute for Clinical and Economic Review's new assessment reports, RealEndpoints' RxScorecard, and the National Comprehensive Cancer Network's evidence blocks. Combine these tools with contracting that does not focus entirely on rebates, and employers may begin to change the rules of a game they will otherwise continue to lose.

> "*The result is that average costs for many drugs are falling. At the same time, consumers are being forced to change medications, sometimes to brands that don't work as well for them.*"

Lowering Drug Prices May Mean Switching Medications

Alison Kodjak

In the following viewpoint, Alison Kodjak discusses the difficult decision that some US consumers are being forced to make. This decision is the substitution of medications that they've taken for years due to high costs. Kodjak explains that this is all due to the all-out war between drug manufacturers and insurance companies, as insurance companies are trying to drive down the costs of expensive drugs, which limits which drugs they'll cover. The subsequent effect of such actions is that some consumers are forced to switch medications to something they can only hope is similar and just as effective as what they were taking before. Kodjak is a health policy correspondent on NPR's Science Desk.

As you read, consider the following questions:

1. How much did Advair sales drop in 2014?
2. By what percentage did drug prices rise in the second quarter of 2015?
3. What have the pharmaceutical companies developed that sometimes help to wipe out a member's copay?

S teve Miller has some customers on offer. Millions of them in fact.

The chief medical officer at Express Scripts, the largest pharmacy benefit manager in the U.S., has been essentially auctioning off his 80 million customers to the drug companies that will give him the best deal.

"Who wants my market share?" Miller says. "Whoever will give me the best price, I will reward you with an enormous amount of market share."

Miller is the most vocal leader in what has become a war on drug prices.

Express Scripts and its rivals including CVS/Caremark and OptumRX manage prescription drug coverage for insurers and employers. They're trying to spark price wars among drugmakers by refusing to pay for some brand-name medications unless they get a big discount.

The result is that average costs for many drugs are falling. At the same time, consumers are being forced to change medications, sometimes to brands that don't work as well for them.

Tim Kilroy is a father of five who runs a business out of his home in Arlington, Mass. Kilroy has attention deficit hyperactivity disorder—ADHD—and he is dependent on his medications to keep his mind, and therefore his business and family life, in order.

"I had tried several drugs," he recalls. "I had tried Concerta; I had tried Adderall. Finding the right dosage can be really challenging."

He spent six years trying medications, adjusting doses, switching and starting over before he and his doctor settled on a long-acting form of Ritalin. He'd finally landed on the drug that worked for him. But about a year ago he switched insurance and the new pharmacy benefit company — United Health Care's Optum subsidiary — refused to pay.

"I thought, 'How dare you,' " Kilroy says. "How dare this company that I pay money to tell me how to manage my health care. I was really, really angry."

He paid for the Ritalin once, but it cost more than $120 a month on top of his insurance premiums. So he asked his doctor to move him to another medication that was covered. Kilroy says it does a good job controlling his ADHD, but the side effects include a swollen prostate that makes it difficult to urinate. So now he's switching insurers again so he can get back on Ritalin.

Kilroy is just one of millions of people affected by this battle between drug companies trying to make as much money as possible and insurers trying to drive down those prices. This year, more than half of all people with insurance will have some medications excluded from coverage, says Ronny Gal, a drug industry analyst at investment firm Alliance Bernstein in New York.

"Drug companies have been pricing their drugs largely along the lines of, you know, whatever you can get away with and still have the patient get the drug," he says. "This year exclusion will become a standard feature of the industry, which is actually quite a shocker for a lot of patients."

Express Scripts pioneered the strategy two years ago, when it announced it would no longer pay for 48 brand-name drugs. Right out of the gate it took on some big-name products, such as Advair — the blockbuster asthma drug made by GlaxoSmithKline, now known as GSK.

Advair's price had risen more than 20 percent in 2013, according to data from SSR Health, a New Jersey-based investment research firm. Then on Jan. 1, 2014, Express Scripts tossed Advair off its drug list and moved its customers to rival asthma drug Symbicort.

The results were immediate. Sales of Advair dropped $1.8 billion that year. The prices of both Advair and Symbicort fell 20 percent in 2014 and are still falling. GSK spokeswoman Jenni Ligday said in a statement that Advair was restored to Express Scripts' formulary last year.

Express Scripts isn't alone. Caremark, Optum and Prime Therapeutics also refuse to pay for some name-brand medications. Dr. David Lassen, the chief medical officer at Prime, which is the pharmacy benefit manager for several Blue Cross and Blue Shield plans, says the company offers an exclusion option to its health plan customers.

He says insurers are knocking drugs off their coverage lists because drug companies have undermined their other efforts to contain costs. In the past, insurers would charge a high copay for expensive drugs to steer customers to cheaper alternatives.

"The pharmaceutical companies have developed member coupons, and many times those coupons wipe out the members' copay for them," Lassen says. "It really kind of circumvents the intended benefit design."

The strategy of refusing to pay for some medications has forced drug companies to offer deep discounts on medications that have competition, according to analyst Richard Evans of SSR Health. While list prices for drugs have continued to rise, Evans wrote in a September report that after discounts drug prices rose only 0.7 percent in the second quarter of 2015 compared with a 4.4 percent increase in the same quarter a year earlier.

For many customers, the changes are a small inconvenience. They have to call their doctors and ask for a prescription for a new brand of painkiller, acne medicine or asthma inhaler. The alternatives often work fine.

But that's not always the case, as Kilroy's situation illustrates.

Oncologist Barbara McAneny, immediate past chairman of the American Medical Association, says very few chemotherapy drugs are excluded from approved drug lists. But the medications used to help patients get through chemo, like painkillers and hormone treatments, are. This complicates her ability to care for her patients.

"Some patients will tolerate one pain medicine, for example, but not another," she says. "One can cause nausea and the other pain medicine doesn't."

If a medication is working, McAneny says it's totally inappropriate for anyone to change that medication and cause the patient to have symptoms.

> *"In 2015 spending on prescription drugs rose by 8.5 percent to US$309.5 billion, compared with a rise of just 1.1 percent for consumer goods and services. Spending for specialty drugs increased by an even heftier 15 percent, on average."*

"Medically Necessary" Drugs Are Increasing Prices Overall

Marcelle Arak and Sheila Tschinkel

In the following viewpoint, Marcelle Arak and Sheila Tschinkel argue that one reason why prescription prices continue to soar is due to more drugs being deemed "medically necessary." This allows drug companies to charge whatever they want because they know consumers need the medicine to survive. The authors propose utilizing the public utilities method, in which an independent federal panel of scientists, medical professionals, and public health experts would help determine the maximum price that could be paid for a drug. Arak is CoBank Professor of Commodities and editor of Global Commodity Issues *at the University of Colorado Denver. Tschinkel has served as resident US Treasury economic advisor in several Eastern European and Central Asian countries and is now on the visiting faculty in economics at Emory University.*

As you read, consider the following questions:

1. By what percentage did spending on prescription drugs rise in 2015?
2. In what situations is the public utilities method frequently used?
3. At what price did a 2014 report put the expense of developing a new drug?

The United States faces a major problem with prescription drug prices. Even as the prices of most goods and services have barely budged in recent years, the cost of drugs has surged.

During the presidential campaign, both Hillary Clinton and Donald Trump cited the high cost of prescription drugs as an issue that needed to be addressed. Most recently, the president-elect took direct aim at the pharmaceutical industry, saying it's "getting away with murder" and arguing "new bidding procedures" are necessary to lower drug prices.

Trump didn't get into specifics about what that would mean, but the most often suggested way to lower drug prices has been to expand the ability of major government buyers, such as Medicare, to negotiate prices.

While such negotiations could result in lower prices, we believe, based on our experience as economists and public policy experts, an alternative using public utility pricing would work better and ensure the discovery and distribution of important new medications.

'Medically Necessary'

The recent drug price data are indeed frightening.

In 2015 spending on prescription drugs rose by 8.5 percent to US$309.5 billion, compared with a rise of just 1.1 percent for consumer goods and services. Spending for specialty drugs increased by an even heftier 15 percent, on average. Individual examples that made big headlines, such as Turing Pharmaceuticals raising the price of Daraprim (a lifesaving drug for people with weakened immune systems) from $13.50 to $750 a tablet, are even more extreme.

In a competitive market, prices of a product are forced down to their costs plus a fair profit. Drug companies, on the other hand, can get away with raising prices without losing customers because the demand for certain medications is insensitive to their cost. If a drug will save your life, you'll probably pay whatever the cost, if you can.

The problem may soon get worse. Last May, Washington state's Medicaid program was ordered to provide the hepatitis C drugs Sovaldi and Harvoni after a court ruled they were "medically necessary." The Washington State Health Care Authority had previously provided Harvoni – which costs $94,500 for an eight-week course of treatment – and Sovaldi – $84,000 for 12 weeks – to only the sickest patients.

Since then, other participants in Medicaid and private insurance plans have filed similar suits. Some states, including Florida, Massachusetts and New York, have already altered their Medicaid programs to pay for such life-preserving expensive drugs.

If "medically necessary" rulings become more common, producers of these drugs will have no need to worry that higher prices will reduce sales. They will be able to charge whatever they want and increase revenue and profit without hurting unit sales because insurance providers will need to make such drugs available to their policy holders.

A Proposed Solution

So what can be done to fix the problem?

Allowing more government agencies to negotiate prices is one option. While this has lowered the prices paid by the Veterans Administration, it may not be the best way to go in a market like the one for many innovative new specialty drugs in which consumers have no good substitutes to choose from.

Economists have shown that negotiated outcomes are not always the most efficient ones. As an example, if the government were to push drug producers too hard in negotiations, the public could get a great deal on prices in the short term but that could end up discouraging the development and testing of new drugs, which would hurt everyone in the long run.

A better approach is to start with a public utilities method, which is frequently used when there is a natural monopoly in production, such as for water or power. In these cases, state and local governments typically allow a company to have a monopoly over the market but also establish regulatory commissions to determine "fair" prices. Such prices take into account current costs, the need for investment in production facilities and the need to earn a rate of return on capital invested.

A wrinkle with drug developers is that they can incur substantial costs in their quest for new medications, including dead-end ideas and extensive testing. A 2014 report put the cost to develop a new drug at $2.6 billion, while others put it at around half that.

Under our proposal, an independent federal panel consisting of scientists, medical professionals, public health experts and economists – perhaps working as part of the FDA approval process and called on when the price of a drug is above a specific threshold – would determine the maximum price a government buyer such as Medicare or Medicaid could pay for a new drug. It could also do the same for existing treatments – for example, it could have turned down Turing's huge Daraprim price hike.

A key element of this idea is that the panel would develop methods to identify and set maximum prices for existing and prospective drugs that cure a serious illness, improve the quality of life, limit contagion or otherwise provide large benefits to society. These procedures would need to make sure that producers of these important new drugs are sufficiently rewarded for those costly efforts.

A Defensible Drug-pricing System

Tough negotiations can help lower how much the government has to pay for its purchases, yet they're not always the optimal way to achieve intended long-term results. With drugs, we definitely need to lower prices but we also need to ensure drug companies can "win" as well to avoid compromising their ability to develop lifesaving medicines.

While economists generally oppose government intervention in a "free market," the current situation cries out for change. It is time to establish a defensible system for pricing drugs, one that both protects the public from price-gouging and encourages the development of new drugs.

Periodical and Internet Sources Bibliography

The following articles have been selected to supplement the diverse views presented in this chapter.

Reed Abelson, "More Insured, but the Choices Are Narrowing," The New York Times, May 12, 2014. https://www.nytimes.com/2014/05/13/business/more-insured-but-the-choices-are-narrowing.html.

Michelle Andrews, "Many Insurers Do Not Cover Weight Loss Drugs," WebMD, Jan. 6, 2015. http://www.webmd.com/health-insurance/news/20150106/many-insurers-do-not-cover-drugs-approved-to-help-people-lose-weight#1.

Felice Freyer, "Hepatitis C patients often have to get sicker before insurance will pay for drugs," The Boston Globe, Apr. 19, 2016. https://www.bostonglobe.com/metro/2016/04/18/insurers-balk-paying-for-hepatitis-drugs/M9Iv0SZcMhHuw1ek3zclLL/story.html.

Seth Ginsberg, "What to Do If You're Denied Coverage for a New Cholesterol Drug You Need," U.S. News, Sept. 9, 2016. http://health.usnews.com/health-news/patient-advice/articles/2016-09-09/what-to-do-if-youre-denied-coverage-for-a-new-cholesterol-drug-you-need.

Lacie Glover, "When Your Insurer Pulls Your Drug Coverage," U.S. News, May 5, 2015. http://health.usnews.com/health-news/patient-advice/articles/2015/05/05/when-your-insurer-pulls-your-drug-coverage.

Scott Gottlieb, "Insurance Plans Are Narrowing Their Drug Coverage," Forbes, Dec. 9, 2015. https://www.forbes.com/sites/scottgottlieb/2015/12/09/why-your-drug-coverage-is-an-increasingly-hollow-benefit/#5da4ad7d2f3e.

Scott Gottlieb, "No, You Can't Keep Your Drugs Either Under Obamacare," Forbes, Dec. 9, 2013. https://www.forbes.com/sites/scottgottlieb/2013/12/09/no-you-cant-keep-your-drugs-either-under-obamacare/#d9c16971f17b.

Sarah Kliff, "Obamacare's narrow networks are going to make people furious — but they might control costs," The Washington Post, Jan. 13, 2014.

https://www.washingtonpost.com/news/wonk/wp/2014/01/13/obamacares-narrow-networks-are-going-to-make-people-furious-but-they-might-control-costs/?utm_term=.394a77f9b9cc.

Philip Moeller, "Medicare woes: Why the meds your doctor prescribes are outrageously expensive," PBS, July 1, 2015.

http://www.pbs.org/newshour/making-sense/medicare-woes-meds-doctor-prescribes-outrageously-expensive.

OPPOSING
VIEWPOINTS®
SERIES

CHAPTER 3

What Are the Ethics Behind Charging Astronomical Prices for Prescription Drugs?

Chapter Preface

To many Americans, it appears that there are absolutely no ethics at play when it comes to soaring costs of prescription medications in the United States. One well-publicized example of that is Martin Shkreli, the founder and CEO of Turing Pharmaceuticals, who hiked up the price of Daraprim, a medication often used to treat HIV and AIDs, from $13.50 per pill to $750 per pill after he bought the rights to the drug.

While Shkreli's actions made national headlines and became a hot topic in the mainstream media, casting him as a ruthless villain, price hikes similar to this one are happening more often than the average person thinks, usually because the average person is not depending on these medications to survive.

The viewpoints in chapter 3 explore the ethics behind charging tremendous prices for pharmaceutical medications. Among the many reasons why a practice like this is unethical, perhaps the most important to consider is the fact that large pharmaceutical companies are profiting from sick people. The pharmaceutical industry thrives on demand, or the need for medications by consumers. These medications are necessary for everyday life, and the drug manufacturers are surely aware of that, and they are able to take advantage of that and charge whatever they want for a pill because they know consumers will pay it to benefit their health or stay alive. And when you consider that Americans spend more on prescription drugs than most other countries, it is clear to see that this is only continuing to become a larger issue in the US. On the other side, pharmaceutical companies claim that the prices are justified when you consider the amount of money that is spent research and development of these medications.

Throughout the course of chapter 3, diverse viewpoints will expose readers to both sides of the issue—consumers and drug manufacturers—who each discuss the ethics of high prescription drug costs. Readers will have the chance to formulate their own opinion based on facts and analysis tied to the debate.

| *"Within limits, ethically acceptable policies should strive to protect patients' access to the drugs that are essential to their medical welfare."*

The Ethics of Pharmaceutical Benefit Management Are Blurry

Stephan L. Burton, Lauren Randel, Karen Titlow, and Ezekiel J. Emanuel

In the following viewpoint, Stephan L. Burton, Lauren Randel, Karen Titlow, and Ezekiel J. Emanuel analyze the ethics of pharmaceutical benefit management. The authors discuss how spending on prescription drugs in the US has risen at double-digit rates within the past decade, and that the ethical goals of medicine need to be analyzed. Overall, the group aims to dissect the six values that should inform pharmacy benefit management, and they ultimately come to the conclusion that benefit caps are unethical and structured tiered copays are reasonable. Burton is a private consultant on issues concerning the compatibility of business and medical values and the ethical structure of pharmaceutical benefits. Randel is an assistant professor in the Department of Psychiatry at Georgetown University Medical Center. Titlow is a project manager at Aetna US Healthcare. Emanuel is chair of the Department of Clinical Bioethics at the Warren G. Magnuson Clinical Center, National Institutes of Health.

As you read, consider the following questions:

1. In what year did pharmaceutical spending increase 19 percent?
2. What is the second value mentioned that should inform pharmacy benefit management?
3. What doesn't traditional fee-for-service (FFS) health insurance offer?

Abstract

Efforts to limit pharmacy costs raise both ethical and economic considerations. Six values should inform pharmacy benefit management: (1) accepting resource constraints; (2) helping the sick; (3) protecting the worst off; (4) respecting autonomy; (5) sustaining trust; and (6) promoting inclusive decision making. Direct controls, such as formularies, step therapy, and prior authorization, can focus limited resources on the sick and worst off. However, direct controls limit autonomy and are administratively burdensome. Indirect controls, such as physician capitation, tiered copayments, and drug benefit caps, align physicians' and patients' interests with resource constraints, respect autonomy, and are administratively efficient. Unfortunately, they deter use based on cost, not medical need; they do not focus cuts on unnecessary or marginal drug use or focus resources on the sick. Budget caps are the least defensible, while tiered copays and physician capitation can be justified if implemented with safeguards. Formularies and step therapy are ethically justifiable if they can be efficiently instituted.

A taxonomy of approaches to control drug costs while respecting the ethical goals of medicine.

Spending on prescription drugs in the United States rose at double-digit rates throughout the past decade, even as the rate of cost increases in other medical services fell to near the overall rate of inflation.[1] Indeed, in 2000 pharmaceutical spending increased 19 percent. Consequently, the percentage of national health care expenditures allocated to prescription drugs rose from about

5.4 percent in 1990 to 8.2 percent in 1999, representing more than $100 billion per year.[2] This trend is expected to continue into the future, largely because of the development and increased use of new drugs and the introduction of pharmacogenomics, rather than because of increased prices for existing drugs.[3]

The increasing burden of prescription drug costs weighs particularly heavily on managed care organizations (MCOs), pharmacy benefit management (PBM) companies, and employers. While recent years have witnessed tighter controls on many medical services, coverage for pharmaceuticals has actually expanded. Traditional fee-for-service (FFS) health insurance did not offer prescription drug coverage; now, mainly as a result of managed care and more effective drugs, such coverage is the norm. Consequently, drugs have become more readily available to more Americans for less out-of-pocket cost, and this trend will increase if a Medicare outpatient drug benefit is enacted. But as drug costs have grown both in absolute terms and as a percentage of overall medical spending, and as potential savings from cuts in other medical expenditures have approached or exceeded acceptable limits, pressure is building to contain pharmaceutical spending.

In response, MCOs, PBMs, and employers have explored various strategies for managing pharmacy benefits. Some of these strategies, such as negotiating with drug companies to bring down prices, seem ethically uncontroversial, although they might be controversial if government entities with dominant market share pursue them. Other approaches, aimed not at reducing prices but limiting drug use (such as prior authorization or tiered copayments), are potentially more problematic.

The more central pharmaceuticals become to health care, the less sense it makes to treat drug benefits as a dispensable frill and the more necessary and important limits become. Limits on drug benefits, and how they are developed and implemented, raise important ethical considerations that must be evaluated as rigorously as their economic impact is. Yet there is almost no ethical analysis of pharmacy benefit management. This paper begins that analysis.

Ethical Values For Pharmacy Benefit Management

PBM policies must seek to balance "mission and margin"—that is, to achieve economic efficiency while respecting, to the extent possible, the ethical goals of medicine. This is difficult. Because of the fragmented nature of the U.S. health care system, MCOs, PBMs, employers, government, and physicians are all involved in the establishment and administration of pharmacy benefits. No stakeholder has absolute responsibility, and all must accept a share of the responsibility to manage these benefits in an ethically justifiable manner. Furthermore, the ways in which pharmacy benefits are financed vary widely. In some cases, it is a benefit like other medical services; in others, it is carved out with a distinct budget. Which stakeholder bears primary responsibility and how the benefit is financed vary by the details of contracts, which require contextualized ethical evaluation. More importantly, the values informing a policy may not be explicitly delineated, making it difficult to identify and compare the ethical implications of pursuing different policies. Thus, it is important to specify (1) the key values that need to be considered in pharmacy benefit management, (2) how different policies realize these values, and (3) which policies seem more or less justifiable.

Fundamental values

No list of ethical values commands universal assent. Yet a few values are widely affirmed as fundamental and cannot be summarily ignored.[4]

Accepting resource constraints

Limits on the coverage and use of drugs are not just an economic necessity but an ethical requirement. There are multiple legitimate claims on resources both between health care and other goods and between various health care services. Resources for health care in general and pharmacy benefits in particular are limited. To satisfy the need for some drugs within the constraints of the resources society is willing to devote to health care may require limits on other services. Similarly, to provide certain necessary health care services may require limits on drug benefits. The ethical challenge is to ensure that these limits are both fair and legitimate.

Helping the sick

The fundamental ethical goal of medicine is to help the sick. It is they who need prescription drugs and who stand to lose the most from unjustifiable barriers to obtaining them. Within limits, ethically acceptable policies should strive to protect patients' access to the drugs that are essential to their medical welfare.

Protecting the worst off

Widely accepted principles of justice require that the welfare of the worst off be specially protected.[5] Thus, pharmacy-benefit management should avoid policies that impose a disproportionate burden on the most vulnerable patients. This does not mean that the claims of the medically worst off are absolute, but they should be given priority when trade-offs are being considered.

Respecting autonomy

Ethically acceptable policies should respect the autonomy of both patients and physicians. Some might place a higher value on convenience or fewer side effects, while others might opt for greater economy. So far as possible, policies should be structured to permit patients to choose among prescription drugs or pharmacy benefit policies according to their own preferences. Similarly, using professional standards, physicians should be free to exercise their judgment about the best drugs to enhance each patient's well-being.

Sustaining trust

Ethically acceptable policies should warrant and sustain patients' trust in their physicians. Such trust is central to the physician-patient relationship.[6] Indeed, it is difficult, if not impossible, for physicians to help patients who do not trust them.[7] Pharmacy benefit management should foster trust and minimize conflicts between physicians' interests and medical responsibilities that could lead patients to perceive them as "double agents" with deeply divided loyalties.[8]

Promoting inclusive decision making

Insurance is inherently a communal activity; it pools resources among a group to benefit the unfortunate. Fundamental to creating a sense of community and shared mission are transparent and inclusive decision-making processes.[9] Physicians and patients are more likely to identify with the goals of an organization if they have a voice in forming and guiding its policies. These processes can make patients and physicians more willing to accept constraints on pharmaceutical use. They can also contribute to accountability for making reasonable decisions by the management organization.[10]

Pragmatic considerations

There is also a practical criterion: It should go without saying that restrictions imposed by a PBM policy in the name of cutting costs should actually achieve that goal. Approaches that end up adding more in administrative and legal expenses than they save in unnecessary medical spending defeat their own purpose, thereby wasting resources at the community's expense.

It is utopian to expect ethical values to identify the single right pharmacy benefit policy. With multiple ethical values involved in allocation decisions, and limited resources, there is no way to avoid conflicts among these values.[11] Considering only the well-being of an individual patient—even the worst-off one—can make all measures to cut drug costs appear objectionable. Saying "yes" to one patient's preference for the latest remedy may mean saying "no" to the more basic needs of others. Providing expensive medications to certain sick patients may drive up overall costs, leaving the poorest and sickest without coverage altogether.

There is more than one way to legitimately balance these ethical values and resolve these conflicts.[12] Ethical analysis can help to identify-policies that may be clearly unethical as well as a range of reasonable policies. It can also elucidate how different policies realize various combinations of values, thereby providing reasons for selecting one approach over another. But ethical values are not the only consideration, especially in an imperfectly just world. Practical and economic considerations cannot be dismissed.

Direct Controls On Drug Use

The following set of policies for controlling pharmaceutical use might be called direct methods. (1) Drugs not included on an organization's formulary (a restricted list of covered drugs) may be covered only under special circumstances or excluded entirely. Exclusions typically target so-called lifestyle drugs, such as contraceptives, treatments for sexual dysfunction, and smoking-cessation aids. (2) Step therapy permits the use of more costly medications only after less expensive drugs with the same indications have been tried and rejected because of therapeutic inefficacy or adverse reactions. (3) Prior authorization may be required before drugs that an organization deems overpriced or over prescribed can be prescribed. (4) Utilization review may be used to weed out unnecessary or conflicting ongoing prescriptions.

Direct controls have distinct advantages, especially by focusing on patient health outcomes, while their ethical shortcomings arise from restrictions on autonomy and administrative burdens. MCOs and PBMs can devote the trained personnel and resources to evaluate thoroughly the efficacy, safety, and comparative indications of medications. They also have the capacity and organizational resources to integrate safety measures into the prescribing and dispensing of drugs. Furthermore, as larger purchasers, they can negotiate price discounts. This enables them to guide pharmacy resources and prescribing practices to promote the best health outcomes. The importance of these advantages will increase as the complexity of the pharmacopoeia increases with the proliferation of medications and the full deployment of pharmacogenomics.

Patients, not profits

What few data exist suggest that concern for patients' welfare is the main motivation for using direct methods to limit utilization.[13] However, if limits were motivated primarily by cost concerns rather than by medical need, patients' welfare might be subverted. Moreover, if physicians and patients merely perceive direct controls as cost-driven, then their trust in the organization that imposes them is undermined. Indeed, since direct controls restrict physicians' and patients' ability to select drugs and increase their dependence on the MCO or PBM, trust is all the more essential. To foster trust and ensure that coverage decisions are seen to reasonably advance patients' welfare and not just savings, direct controls should be developed through an inclusive, transparent decision making procedure. Giving physicians and patients a voice in establishing and structuring controls on pharmaceutical use can restore some of the autonomy that such controls take away, albeit collectively rather than individually. In dispersed networks that lack a sense of community, shared decision-making procedures might also help to foster such a sense. Although physicians are now well represented on committees that evaluate pharmacy benefits for MCOs, patient participation is rare.

Administrative burden

Combined with restricting autonomy, the main disadvantages of direct methods relate to administrative burden and inflexibility. Many physicians work with several health plans. For them, the administrative burden of abiding by the plans' differing formularies, step requirements, and prior authorization procedures can be both costly and time-consuming. Administrative hassles alienate physicians from the MCO or PBM and reduce their already limited time for seeing patients. In addition, prior authorization and utilization review are administratively cumbersome and costly for MCOs and PBMs. Such was the experience that persuaded United HealthCare to abandon prior authorization requirements for hospitalization in 1999.[14]

Disruption of drug regimens

Direct controls also may disrupt already established medications for new enrollees, if they are required to start all over with new drugs mandated by their new plan, and for continuing enrollees when mandated drugs change. This is not a trivial problem, since such switching can occur frequently, even annually, depending on new discounts negotiated with drug manufacturers.

Formulary exclusion

Finally, certain drugs or classes of drugs that arguably possess genuine medical value may be targeted for exclusion from formularies for noncost but value-laden reasons. For example, many organizations exclude all smoking-cessation products, despite their considerable preventive value. Similarly, the designation "lifestyle drug" does not simply express an objective and uncontroversial scientific fact but, rather, embodies subjective and disputable value judgments that are used to keep drugs off of formularies, raising ethical concerns as well.[15]

Indirect Controls On Drug Use

Indirect methods for limiting drug use include the following. (1) Physician capitation for prescription drug costs passes financial incentives to control drug spending on to physicians. They are paid a set allowance for each patient that must cover the patient's yearly prescription drug costs, with any excess coming out of the physician's own pocket. (2) Patient copayments pass financial incentives on to patients. In tiered systems, the amount of the copay varies. Typically, patients might pay $5 for generic drugs; $10 for brand name equivalents; and $25, or a percentage of retail costs, for medications that are not included on an insurer's approved formulary. (3) Caps on pharmacy benefits require patients to pay the full cost of all medications once their drug spending exceeds a set amount per quarter or per year.

These methods are not mutually exclusive; they may be used in various combinations. For example, tiered copayments may be imposed within formularies.

Indirect controls address the problems of autonomy and administrative burdens related to direct controls through the use of incentives and financial limits within which patients and physicians exercise free choice. Indirect controls pass along costs to physicians and patients, while freeing them of paperwork hassles and giving them the opportunity to exercise their own choices among drugs.

Align financial interests

By providing an incentive—but not a mandate—to reduce costs and opt for cheaper medications, indirect controls tend to align the financial interests of patients and physicians with those of the MCO or PBM. Physician capitation gives physicians an incentive to resist excessive consumer demand for expensive or over prescribed drugs. This is no small feat; studies have shown just how hard it is to get physicians to focus on drug costs in prescribing decisions, how susceptible they are to drug detailing, and how readily they yield to patients' demands.[16]

Similarly, tiered copayments and benefit caps can make patients more appreciative of the virtues of generic drugs and less heavily advertised medications because these drugs make a difference to their own budgets. For example, patients with strep throat can decide whether the convenience of a single daily dose of a brand name antibiotic for five days is worth the extra cost compared with taking a generic four times a day for ten days. Also, because the patient is the ultimate decision maker, tiered copays and caps avoid the appearance of an unethical conflict of interest and pose less of a threat to trust in the MCO and PBM than direct controls do. To the extent that capitation, tiered copays, and benefit caps control overall costs, they can serve the cause of distributive justice.

Disrupt physician-patient relationship

While respecting autonomy and reducing hassles, indirect controls raise different problems. First, if the organization's financial incentives are passed along through physician capitation, the problem of distrust resurfaces in the relationships between physicians and their patients.[17]

More importantly, indirect controls are a blunt, nondiscriminating instrument of cost control. The incentives exert pressure on use in proportion to cost, regardless of medical necessity, threatening patients' well-being, especially that of poorer patients. Ideally, physicians and patients would respond to these incentives by focusing resources on the most medically necessary drugs. But in reality, physicians see patients one at a time and do not have the resources to determine which drugs for which patients will achieve optimal health outcomes. Also, medically irrelevant factors could be influential in physicians' prescribing decisions. They might be influenced by how demanding patients are, putting sicker but meeker patients at risk of receiving less treatment.[18] In addition, worrying about exceeding their capitation, physicians might stint on preventive medications, such as expensive cholesterol-lowering statins, because the health benefits lie in the future when the patient could easily be with a different health plan or physician.

Target the worst-off patients

Tiered copays and budget caps target patients, not physicians. While patients may be knowledgeable about the trade-off of convenience and cost and about the comparative tolerability of side effects, they lack professional training in the appropriate use of medications for particular illnesses, drug interactions, how drugs might affect other illnesses, and especially about the consequence of forgoing medications because of expense. To the extent that they are less qualified than physicians are to make well-informed decisions about use, health can suffer. Recognizing this, some health plans and PBMs offer decision tools and advice about drugs directly to patients.

What is worse, tiered copays and caps may deter patients in proportion to their ability to pay rather than their medical need. In this regard, budget caps are much more worrisome because they amount to a 100 percent copay once expenditures exceed a certain level. Recent studies have shown that copays are effective in reducing pharmaceutical use.[19] But this is cause for celebration only if the reductions come primarily from those who might be tempted to use drugs unnecessarily or irresponsibly, rather than from patients who need them but cannot afford them. Indeed, tiered copays and especially benefit caps target the sickest; the sicker a person is and the more medications he or she needs, the higher the costs. A 1998 Harvard Pilgrim Health Care study found that 14 percent of its Medicare patients would exceed a proposed annual pharmaceutical cap of $800.[20] It is precisely these patients who are sickest, most in need of medication, who would be harmed the most by caps.

Create incentives to accept only the healthiest

Finally, these indirect controls create adverse selection incentives. Physician capitation creates an incentive to accept only the healthiest patients, who are least likely to exceed their set allowance, while refusing the elderly and the seriously or chronically ill. Unless payments are risk-adjusted, capitation threatens to limit the health care options of the medically worst-off patients. Similarly, systems using benefit caps and tiered copays create an incentive for a "race to the bottom" among MCOs and PBMs. If higher benefit caps or smaller copays are likely to attract high-risk, high-cost patients with expensive pharmaceutical requirements, health plans will have the incentive to alter their benefits to deter the riskiest and most costly members from enrolling. Because of adverse selection when offering an un-limited drug benefit, Harvard Pilgrim has instituted a drug benefit cap. This forces competing MCOs and PBMs to do the same. Tragically, then, high copayments and low benefit caps can harm not only the most vulnerable members of one MCO or PBM, but the sick patients in an entire marketplace.

Tiered copays have one unique problem: MCOs and PBMs may end up subsidizing drugs whose higher prices are not, in their judgment, justified by corresponding therapeutic superiority. Even the highest tier of a typical three-tier copay system may represent only a nominal contribution to the cost of marginally beneficial, but highly expensive, drugs. For example, patients who are willing to pay a $25–$35 copay for Cox-2 inhibitors in preference to standard anti-inflammatory medications will incur an additional bill for thousands of dollars over a typical course of treatment. This cost is borne not just by the insurer but by the purchaser and fellow patients.

Recommendations For Ethical Pharmacy Benefit Policy

Which pharmaceutical benefit management policies are ethically the most defensible? Which are the least so?

Tiered copayments

If emphasis is placed on physician and patient autonomy as well as administrative simplicity, then indirect controls are preferable. Among these, tiered copayments can be carefully structured to be ethically justifiable. To minimize their threat to patient welfare, the tiers should be structured primarily according to medical benefit rather than cost. The lowest tier should include expensive drugs when they are medically necessary, while the highest tier could be reserved for drugs with cheaper alternatives and nonessential "lifestyle" drugs. Because designating these latter types of drugs will be controversial, it is best to create an inclusive decision-making process, with patient representatives on pharmacy and therapeutics (P&T) committees and other relevant decision-making bodies.

Such ethical considerations are likely to necessitate changes in the design of tiered copay systems. Tiered systems now tend to charge more for brand-name medications, even when there is no generic alternative, and more costly medications, even when they are judged medically necessary.[21] According to a recent survey, 27 percent of MCOs charge a higher copayment even when they approve a medical exception for a third-tier drug.[22]

No caps on pharmacy benefits

Conversely, caps on pharmacy benefits should be ruled out under all circumstances. They raise clear and seemingly irresolvable ethical problems. They are directed at the sickest and poorest patients, not at medically inappropriate use of drugs; they empower the least qualified to make drug decisions; and they strongly encourage adverse selection among MCOs and PBMs.

Pharmacy benefit entitlement?

This would seem to imply that insurers and employers have an ethical obligation to provide a pharmacy benefit. That is, if benefit caps are unethical, then surely no drug benefit—a cap of zero—is unethical. While this is not the place for a comprehensive defense, we believe that there is a persuasive argument for a universal entitlement to some health care.[23] The failure of the U.S. government to provide it is an ethical lapse, not an ethical argument against such an entitlement. In weighing what health care services people should be entitled to, drugs would surely be included. Their effectiveness in preventing and curing diseases and relieving debilitating symptoms and disabilities makes their contribution to health outcomes comparable to or better than other services that are routinely considered essential and covered by insurance, such as office visits, surgical procedures, and some screening tests. While some limit on drug benefits is reasonable, a zero drug benefit is unjustifiable. Such a view seems implicit in the discussion of a Medicare drug benefit.

Physician capitation

Like tiered copays, physician capitation can be structured to be ethically justifiable mainly by minimizing the threat to trust. As we have argued regarding other forms of physician capitation, safeguards exist that can minimize these threats, including risk adjustment, stop-loss provisions, spreading the capitation among a large group of physicians, combining the capitation with guidelines, and monitoring underuse.[24] Ethical considerations suggest the need to restructure current pharmacy capitation policies to make them justifiable.

In general, the ethical risks of direct controls on pharmaceutical use may be more easily addressed, but the administrative hassles may be more difficult to overcome. The concern that MCOs and PBMs focus solely on cutting costs can be addressed by an inclusive decision-making process. If decisions about the establishment and structure of formularies are made on purely medical grounds with the genuine participation of both physicians and patients, potential threats to patient welfare, autonomy, and community can be minimized. MCOs and PBMs can be held accountable.[25] Such participation in the decision-making process is desirable, whatever policies are ultimately chosen. This gives representation to the values of those who must live with the decisions made and can educate physicians and patients about the reality of the trade-offs involved and the need to choose wisely and fairly among them.

But not all of the direct controls are equivalent. Prior authorization and utilization review create more administrative hassles for physicians and alienation of physicians and patients. They seem more intrusive and punitive, explicitly designed to catch overuse. In contrast, formularies and step therapies establish parameters and allow physicians and patients to work within them. To overcome the problem of physicians' having to contend with multiple formularies, it may be worth exploring the possibility of having different MCOs and PBMs in one marketplace collaborate on a formulary or an agreed-upon set of step therapies. While this cooperation might raise antitrust concerns, it also can present significant advantages.

Every decision to allocate scarce medical resources raises ethical as well as economic considerations. Too often ethical considerations go unrecognized or even ignored, in part because the ethical values and trade-offs have not been explicitly delineated for policymakers. This seems to be what has occurred as MCOs, PBMs, and employers scramble to implement policies to control exploding pharmacy costs.

But ethical analysis can illuminate which policies best reflect specific ethical values and ways of structuring policies to avoid certain ethical problems or realize other ethical values. Our analysis suggests that benefit caps are unethical; that if autonomy is emphasized, properly structured tiered copays are reasonable; and that if drugs are used to optimize health outcomes, especially for the vulnerable, then step therapy or restrictive formularies are most justifiable.

Endnotes

1. Employee Benefit Research Institute, "Prescription Drug Costs Up Sharply—but Still Small Overall," Press Release 470 (Washington: EBRI, 1999); and Consumer Price Index—All Urban Consumers (Washington: U.S. Department of Commerce, Bureau of Labor Statistics, 2000).

2. S. Smith et al., "The Next Decade of Health Spending: A New Outlook," *Health Affairs* (July/Aug 1999): 86–95.

3. Health Care Financing Administration, "National Health Expenditures Projection Table 12a: Prescription Drug Expenditures and Average Annual Percent Change, by Source of Funds: Selected Calendar Years 1970–2008" (Washington: HCFA, 2000); and E.F.X. Hughes, "A Perspective on the Future of American Health Care: The Increasingly Central Role of Pharmacy," *Proceedings of Pharmacy Benefit Management: Balancing Clinical and Financial Objectives* (HAP/AFHS Conference, Dearborn, Michigan, 13 April 1999), 1–3.

4. T.L. Beauchamp and J.F. Childress, *Principles of Biomedical Ethics,* 4th ed. (New York: Oxford University Press, 1994).

5. J. Rawls, *A Theory of Justice* (Cambridge, Mass.: Harvard University Press, 1971) and N. Daniels, *Just Health Care* (Cambridge, U.K.: Cambridge University Press, 1985).

6. D. Mechanic, "The Functions and Limitations of Trust in the Provision of Medical Care," *Journal of Health Politics, Policy and Law* 23, no. 4 (1998): 661–686.

7. D. Mechanic and M. Rosenthal, "Responses of HMO Medical Directors to Trust Building in Managed Care," *Milbank Quarterly* 77, no. 3 (1999): 283–303.

8. M. Angell, "The Doctor as Double Agent," *Journal of the Kennedy Institute of Ethics* 3, no. 3 (1993): 279–286.

9. E.J. Emanuel, "Justice and Managed Care: Four Principles for the Just Allocation of Health care Resources," *Hastings Center Report* 30, no. 3 (2000): 8–16; and N. Daniels and J.E. Sabin, *Setting Fair Limits: Can We Learn to Share Medical Resources?* (New York: Oxford University Press, forthcoming), chap. 6.

10. N. Daniels and J. Sabin, "The Ethics of Accountability in Managed Care Reform," *Health Affairs* (Sep/Oct 1998): 50–64.

11. L. Randel et al., "How Managed Care Can Be Ethical," *Health Affairs* (July/Aug 2001): 43–56.

12. Ibid.

13. K. Titlow et al., "Drug Coverage Decisions: The Role of Dollars and Values," *Health Affairs* (Mar/Apr 2000): 240–247.

14. "Big HMO to Give Decisions on Care Back to Doctors," *New York Times*, 9 November 1999, A1.

15. Ibid.

16. T.H. Gallagher et al., "How Do Physicians Respond to Patients' Requests for Costly, Unindicated Services?" *Journal of General Internal Medicine* **12**, no. 11 (1997): 663–668; R. Gonzales, J.F. Steiner, and M.A. Sande, "Antibiotic Prescribing for Adults with Colds, Upper Respiratory Tract Infections, and Bronchitis by Ambulatory Care Physicians," *Journal of the American Medical Association* **278**, no. 11 (1997): 901–904; and A.C. Nyquist et al., "Antibiotic Prescribing for Children with Colds, Upper Respiratory Tract Infections, and Bronchitis," *Journal of the American Medical Association* **279**, no. 11 (1998): 875–877.

17. S.D. Pearson, J.E. Sabin, and E.J. Emanuel, "Ethical Guidelines for Physician Compensation Based on Capitation," *New England Journal of Medicine* **339**, no. 10 (1998): 689–693.

18. M. Monane et al., "Improving Prescribing Patterns for the Elderly through an Online Drug Utilization Review Intervention: A System Linking the Physician, Pharmacist, and Computer," *Journal of the American Medical Association* **280**, no. 14 (1998): 1249–1252; D.M. Berwick, "Quality of Health Care, Part 5: Payment by Capitation and the Quality of Care," *New England Journal of Medicine* **335**, no. 16 (1996): 1227–1231; and Y. Twersky and H. Lipsky, "Capitation and the Medicaid Elderly," *Annals of Internal Medicine* **121**, no. 6 (1994): 469–470.

19. A.L. Hillman et al., "Financial Incentives and Drug Spending in Managed Care," *Health Affairs* (Mar/Apr 1999): 189–200; and B. Stuart and C. Zacker, "Who Bears the Burden of Medicaid Copayment Policies?" *Health Affairs* (Mar/Apr 1999): 201–212.

20. D.B. Moskowitz, "Marketplace: Harvard Pilgrim Looks to Tighter Controls to Turn Unexpected Red Ink Back to Black," *Medicine and Health* **53**, no. 21, Supp. 1–2 (1999).

21. "Special Report—Three-Tier Co-Payment Plans: Design Considerations and Effectiveness," *Drug Benefit Trends* **11**, no. 9 (1999): 43–52.

22. Scott-Levin, *Managed Care Formulary Drug Audit* (Newtown, Pa.: Scott-Levin, Fall 1999).

23. Daniels, *Just Health Care*.

24. Pearson et al., "Ethical Guidelines for Physician Compensation."

25. Daniels and Sabin, "The Ethics of Accountability in Managed Care Reform."

| *"Since 2004, one out of every 10 dollars expended on health care in the United States has been for prescription drugs."*

Americans Spend More on Prescriptions Than Most

Steve Morgan and Jae Kennedy

In the following viewpoint, Steve Morgan and Jae Kennedy break down data from the Commonwealth Fund 2007 International Health Policy Survey, as well as data from the Organization for Economic Cooperation and Development (OECD) and other sources to analyze various aspects of pharmaceutical drugs in seven countries: Australia, Canada, Germany, the Netherlands, New Zealand, the United Kingdom, and the United States. The data and analysis are broken down by various categories and aspects pertaining to prescription drugs, including use, access, cost, and more. Morgan is associate professor at the School of Population and Public Health at the University of British Columbia. Kennedy is associate professor of Health Policy and Administration at Washington State University and a faculty affiliate at the Centre for Health Services and Policy Research at the University of British Columbia.

"Prescription Drug Accessibility and Affordability in the United States and Abroad," by Steve Morgan and Jae Kennedy, The Commonwealth Fund, June 2010. Reprinted by permission.

As you read, consider the following questions:

1. What country is generally more likely than residents of other surveyed countries to use prescription drugs?
2. What country is much more likely than residents of the other countries to report out-of-pocket spending in excess of $1,000 in the previous year?
3. Which two countries in this study did not ensure universal access to drug coverage?

Background

Within a generation, prescription drugs have become a major component of health systems worldwide. They are central to most aspects of medicine, from primary care to specialized treatment.

Since 2004, one out of every 10 dollars expended on health care in the United States has been for prescription drugs.[1] While this may sound modest, prescription drugs accounted for only 4.7 percent of total U.S. health care expenditures in 1980 and just 5.6 percent in 1990.[2] Thus, prescription drugs nearly doubled as a share of U.S. health care spending in little more than a decade. Increases in spending per person also have occurred in other countries—although far less rapidly. As a result, the U.S. stands out for much higher spending per person, with the gap between the U.S and other countries increasing. U.S. spending was the highest among the seven countries in this study; as of 2005, the U.S. reached $790 per capita compared with $599 in Canada, the next highest country, and $292 in New Zealand. As illustrated, the other countries have each experienced much slower annual growth rates.

While prescription drugs can improve patients' health, their rising prominence in health care systems has come with access, safety, and cost challenges. Pharmaceutical policy needs to balance goals related to the availability and safety of medicines, the accessibility and appropriate use of treatment options, and the affordability and sustainability of costs borne by individuals and by the system as a whole. As we will discuss, the experience of several countries shows that a coordinated national pharmaceutical policy can support achievement of these goals.

Using data from the Commonwealth Fund 2007 International Health Policy Survey, as well as data from the Organization for Economic Cooperation and Development (OECD) and other sources, we sought to gauge pharmaceutical policy performance for the seven participating countries: Australia, Canada, Germany, the Netherlands, New Zealand, the United Kingdom, and the United States.[3] We focus our attention in this issue brief on issues of accessibility and cost:

- *Accessibility:* Are patients able to access necessary medicines regardless of age, income, or other factors?
- *Cost:* Does the cost of prescribed medicines represent a fair and manageable burden for individuals and the system overall?
- *Payment Policies:* How can country policies help assure access and affordability?

Use of Pharmaceuticals

Americans are generally more likely than residents of other surveyed countries to use prescription drugs, according to the 2007 results. The percentage of survey respondents reporting using one or more prescription drugs in the past year ranged from 46 percent in Germany to 60 percent in the U.S. The percentage of survey respondents reporting using four or more prescription drugs ranged from a low of about 13 percent in Germany to a high of 17 percent in the U.S. and Australia.

Underlying these cross-national differences in reported prescription drug use are patterns of use by age, health status, and income that reveal potentially important differences in medical care and equity of access.

Differences by Age and Health Status

The likelihood that older and sicker adults will use prescription drugs is roughly comparable in all seven countries. For example, Americans age 65 and older are about as likely to use one or more prescriptions per year as similarly aged persons in the other six countries, and Americans with two or more chronic conditions are about as likely to fill one or more prescriptions as persons with two or more chronic conditions in those countries.

By contrast, younger and healthier Americans use prescription drugs more often than do their counterparts in the six other countries. U.S. adults ages 30 to 49 and 50 to 64 are more likely to use at least one prescription than similarly aged people in the other countries, though in the former of these two groupings, there is little difference between Americans and the Australians and Dutch.

Americans with one chronic illness or none were more likely to fill one or more prescriptions than were persons of similar health status in all other countries except the Netherlands (where differences with Americans were not significant). It thus appears that doctors in the U.S. have a greater propensity to prescribe drugs for relatively healthy people than do doctors in the other countries. It is perhaps notable that the U.S. and New Zealand are the only countries that permit direct-to-consumer advertising of prescription drugs, and that the intensity of the practice is far greater in the U.S. Resulting patient requests for prescriptions may therefore help explain the high use of medicines in the U.S., including among relatively young or healthy populations.[4]

Equity of Access

While cross-national differences in prescription drug use are suggestive of differences in medical practice patterns, differences across population groups within countries suggest possible inequities in medical care. Researchers in many countries have documented a positive relationship between income and health status.[5] The poor are generally less healthy and thus would be expected—with equal access—to use medications more frequently. This expected pattern emerges in five of the seven countries. In Australia, Canada, the Netherlands, New Zealand, and the U.K., the lowest income group studied was substantially more likely than the highest income group to have used a prescription drug. In the United States and Germany, however, there was little difference between those with below-average income and those with average income. Indeed, in the U.S., income makes virtually no difference in using at least one prescription medicine.

The lack of difference between people with below- and above-average incomes could perhaps be seen as an indicator of equity. However, given the widely documented association between income and health, this pattern suggests either low-income Americans are not able to access medicines they need, that higher-income Americans may be receiving more medicines than they need, or both. Notably, U.S. adults with below-average income were far more likely than those with above- average income to rate their health as fair or poor (31% vs. 10%) and to have been diagnosed with least one of seven chronic conditions (63% vs. 48%). It is worth noting that the country that has the highest rate of prescription drug use by those with above-average incomes is the United States, while people with lower-than-average incomes in four of the survey countries have higher rates of use than in this the U.S.

Financial Barriers and Prescription Drug-Skipping

Reported rates of cost-related nonadherence to prescribed treatments add further evidence of inequity in access to prescription drugs in the U.S. Despite higher rates of prescription drug use in the U.S., Americans are more likely than residents of the other countries to report having left prescriptions unfilled or skipped doses because of cost, and Americans with low income report the highest rates of such financial barriers.

The percent of the population reporting not filling a prescription or skipping a dose because of cost during the previous 12 months ranged from 2 percent in the Netherlands to 23 percent in the U.S. With or without adjusting for sex, age, income, and health status, residents of all other countries studied were significantly less likely (50 percent or more) than Americans to report these financial barriers to use of prescriptions.

The higher extent to which U.S. adults go without prescriptions or skip doses because of costs appears in all income groups. High-income Americans were as or more likely to report cost-related barriers to medicine use than all income groups combined in every country except Australia. Low-income Australians were the only income group in any another country to report financial barriers more frequently than high-income Americans. This likely reflects gaps in coverage and high cost-sharing that even insured Americans often experience.

Low-income Americans were at particularly high risk of cost-related nonadherence. More than one-third (34%) of low-income Americans reported not filling prescriptions or skipping doses during the past 12 months, far beyond the rate among low-income adults in any of the other countries. Indeed, in several countries—the Netherlands, Germany, and the U.K.—there were few differences between below-average and above-average income groups in going without medications because of cost. The steep differences in the U.S. between below-average, middle-income, and above-average-income adults likely reflects differences in insurance protection, with rising rates of uninsured and underinsured among low- and middle-income families.[6]

Affordability

The affordability of prescription drugs can be considered either at the level of individual out-of-pocket expenses or at the level of overall costs to the system. We present both.

Out-of-Pocket Costs

Even with their higher rate of unfulfilled prescriptions, Americans are much more likely than residents of the other countries to report out-of-pocket spending in excess of $1,000 in the previous year. At

13.2 percent of the population reporting such high out-of-pocket costs, no other country comes close to the U.S. on this measure. The next highest share of population paying $1,000 or more in out-of-pocket for prescription drugs is 5.7 percent and is found in Canada where—like the U.S.—many people have no private or public drug coverage.[7]

In countries with comprehensive drug benefit programs that have low copayments—Germany, the Netherlands, New Zealand, and the U.K.—fewer than 3 percent of the population had out-of-pocket costs of $1,000 or more for prescription drugs. In Australia, where drug coverage is universal but comes with relatively high copayments (AUD$30) for general beneficiaries, about 5 percent of the population reported out-of-pocket spending in excess of $1,000.

As was the case with patterns of medicine use, within-country variation in high out-of-pocket costs is as important as cross-national differences. The likelihood of facing high out-of-pocket costs is higher among those with chronic disease in most countries. But the impact of health status on out-of-pocket expense is most significant in the U.S., where more than one of five people with two or more chronic conditions face $1,000 or more in out-of-pocket prescription costs.

Total Spending per Person and Prices

As noted earlier, despite access barriers and high out-of-pocket costs, total pharmaceutical spending per person is far higher in the U.S. than in the six comparison countries. Moreover, in the past decade pharmaceutical expenditures per capita have grown faster in the United States than in the comparison countries, adjusted for general inflation. By 2005, U.S. pharmaceutical spending per person was 30 percent higher than in Canada and nearly twice the level of spending in New Zealand. In total, the U.S. spent more than $234 billion on prescription drugs in 2005.

It is extraordinarily difficult to assess cross-national differences in drug prices because standard doses and package sizes vary

Support for Policy Changes

About half of Americans (54%) report currently taking a prescription drug, and a large majority of them (72%) say their prescriptions are very or somewhat easy to afford. However, about a quarter (24%) say paying for their drugs is difficult, and the share facing difficulties rises among those with low incomes (33%) or currently taking four or more prescription drugs (38%), and is highest for those in fair or poor health (43%).

These are among the findings from the August Kaiser Health Tracking Poll, which expands on findings from earlier this year looking at prescription drug costs. The new poll finds strong majorities of the public support a wide range of policy actions to lower the costs of prescription drugs. At least seven in 10 support each of these four potential policy changes:

- 86 percent support requiring drug companies to release information on how they set prices, an idea proposed in legislatures in several states, including majorities of Democrats (90%), Republicans (82%), and independents (84%);
- 83 percent support allowing the government to negotiate with drug companies to lower prices for people with Medicare, including majorities of Democrats (93%), Republicans (74%), and independents (83%);
- 76 percent support limiting how much drug companies can charge for high-cost drugs for illnesses such as hepatitis or cancer, including majorities of Democrats (79%), Republicans (70%), and independents (77%); and
- 72 percent support allowing Americans to buy prescription drugs imported from Canada, including majorities of Democrats (69%), Republicans (75%), and independents (76%).

"Most Say They Can Afford Their Prescription Drugs, But One in Four Say Paying Is Difficult, Including More Than Four in Ten People Who Are Sick," by Katie Smith and Amy Jeter, Kaiser Family Foundation, August 20, 2015.

from country to country and are seldom taken into account in price comparisons. Moreover, negotiated discounts between manufacturers and insurers are ubiquitous in the U.S., whereas such discounts were relatively rare in most other countries until very recently. Because the use of negotiated discounts to secure savings has the effect of driving up the list prices of drugs, there is little doubt that uninsured persons in the U.S. pay higher prices for prescription medicines than patients (or governments) pay in other countries. However, prices for drugs that do not involve discounting—e.g., prices for generic drugs—are actually lower in the U.S. than in other countries. Thus, cross-national differences in drug spending likely result from the combined effects of higher use of medicines in the U.S., use of newer, more costly therapeutic options, and higher prices paid by the uninsured or underinsured.

International Policy Strategies for Access and Affordability: Insights for the United States

The findings concerning the accessibility and affordability of prescription drugs in the United States are troubling. Despite the fact that the U.S. spends more on prescriptions per person than any other country studied here, rates of patients' nonadherence to prescribed treatment because of cost considerations are highest in the U.S.; within-country utilization patterns suggest income-related disparities in access in the U.S. (and, to a lesser extent, in Canada and Australia); and patients in the U.S. face higher out-of-pocket costs than in any other country, especially patients with chronic illness.

These findings concerning accessibility and affordability of medicines in the U.S. likely stem from the incomplete nature of health and pharmaceutical coverage and the lack of coordinated purchasing policies regarding prescription medications. Studies repeatedly find negative health and total cost effects from high out-of-pocket prescription costs for patients with chronic disease and other health concerns, with high rates of cost-related nonadherence to prescribed treatments. These cost effects result from complications and higher emergency department use that could have been prevented with adequate medication regimens. [8] In other countries, a focus on health and drug benefit policy designed to provide universal access to essential treatments works together with group purchasing and pricing policies to provide affordable access at the patient and population level.

Ensuring Access

Affordability of medicines for individual patients is facilitated by policies that limit cost-sharing for covered individuals and design benefits with incentives to use effective, essential medications. This is substantiated not just by the evidence presented above, but by a growing body of research showing that even modest levels of cost- sharing can lead patients to cease or skimp on the use of essential and nonessential drugs alike.[9]

All countries in this study except the U.S. and Canada ensure universal access to drug coverage. Most of these countries do so with relatively low cost-sharing by patients, especially for vulnerable populations (e.g., children, the elderly, the chronically ill, and the poor). The Canadian system of public drug coverage is comparable to that of the U.S., with public coverage targeted (primarily) to the elderly and social assistance recipients, as well as a mix of privately insured and uninsured among other population groups. However, public programs finance a greater share of total prescription drug costs in Canada than in the U.S. (overall and for specific beneficiary groups such as the elderly).

Just like access to primary care, ensuring access to essential medicines—without barriers such as those due to geography, age, income, or employment—can be cost-effective when viewed from health system and societal levels.[10]

Managing Pharmaceutical Costs

In providing universal coverage, countries also can manage expenditures on medicines by two mechanisms: 1) the processes and criteria used to determine which medicines will be covered and with what cost-sharing; and 2) relative pricing policies and negotiations concerning the price of medicines.

Formularies and related price negotiations are commonplace in the U.S., where major private insurers and some public buyers exercise buying power on behalf of population subgroups. Different formularies may apply to different patients, depending upon their insurer. By contrast, in countries that have universal coverage and a commitment to base that coverage and cost-sharing on best available evidence, there is a single formulary and physicians have no need to sort out which formulary applies to which patient.

In most countries studied, information about the comparative clinical- and cost-effectiveness of medicines is systematically assessed to determine which medicines should or should not be subsidized, and at what level of coverage. In the U.K., the system is governed by a negative formulary, meaning that all medicines are eligible for public subsidy unless identified as a nonbenefit. Therefore, the National Institute for Health and Clinical Excellence focuses its assessments on controversial medicines. In other countries, every medicine is appraised to determine whether it should be subsidized and at what rate.[11] Such comparative assessment review can help spur both the development and adoption of innovative and cost-effective medicines, as well as target use where medications are effective for particular patients.[12]

Once a medicine is deemed to be a candidate for coverage under a universal drug benefit system, a key consideration is the price that can be charged. In Australia and Germany, for example, prices paid by insurers for virtually all products are controlled by reference to the prices of comparable alternatives—a system called reference pricing. In Canada, prices are limited in comparison to those charged in seven comparator countries (including the U.S.). The Netherlands uses both reference pricing and price ceilings based on averages paid in comparison countries.

Increasingly, however, drug benefit managers are negotiating contracts with drug manufacturers so that acceptable prices can be secured while providing the manufacturer with certain guarantees of market share or of pricing confidentiality. Consider public benefits in New Zealand, which operate with a national formulary managed by the Pharmaceutical Management Agency of New Zealand (PHARMAC). Informed by independent and systematic review of the comparative cost-effectiveness of all products that seek public subsidy, PHARMAC uses a variety of supplier contracts and coverage policies to meet annual budget targets for public expenditures on medicines. PHARMAC negotiates rebates on list prices, uses sole-source contracts for supply of off-patent drugs, and engages in other deals with suppliers to procure drugs at the most competitive prices possible. All of the tools PHARMAC applies are used to various extents by drug plans in the U.S.; but when applied universally their effectiveness is clear.

Spending on medicines in New Zealand has grown very slowly, adjusted for general inflation. Indeed, if from 1995 to 2005 U.S. spending per capita had grown at a rate comparable to New Zealand, per capita pharmaceutical spending in the U.S. would be approximately $510 in 2005, which is $280 less than was actually the case. The total savings implied by such a thought experiment is on the order of $80 billion in 2005 alone. Potential savings of nearly that magnitude would also be found by comparison to Germany or the Netherlands, where national formulary management occurs despite the fact that the underlying health systems are based on social insurance models with many competing insurers.[13]

Conclusions

Pharmaceuticals are an essential component of health care, and ensuring appropriate access to them can be a cost-effective way of treating illness and promoting the health of the population. At the same time, use of information to guide and inform benefit designs and pricing policies can help moderate cost increases while assuring access to effective medications, including new products.

The Patient Protection and Affordable Care Act of 2010 will expand prescription drug access mainly by requiring most U.S. citizens and legal residents to obtain health insurance and by defining prescription coverage as an essential insurance benefit. [14] Because uninsured Americans are currently more likely than their insured counterparts to go without prescribed medications, this should improve medication adherence at the population level.[15] While an expansion of this sort will likely drive up per capita drug expenditures, systems of universal, regulated social insurance guided by evidence-based formulary management— such as is seen in Germany and the Netherlands—are ones from which U.S. policymakers may take important lessons. One message from abroad is clear: sustainability, affordability, and equity in pharmaceutical coverage will require commitment to universality and openness to a more coordinated system of financing and evidence-based expenditure management.

Endnotes

1. M. Hartman, A. Martin, P. McDonnell et al., "National Health Spending in 2007: Slower Drug Spending Contributes to Lowest Rate of Overall Growth Since 1998," *Health Affairs,* Jan./Feb. 2009 28(1):246–61.

2. Organization for Economic Cooperation and Development, *OECD Health Data 2008: Statistics and Indicators for 30 Countries* (CD-ROM) (Paris: OECD, 2008).

3. S. Morgan, J. Kennedy, K. Boothe et al., "Toward an Understanding of High Performance Pharmaceutical Policy Systems: A 'Triple-A' Framework and Example Analysis," *The Open Health Services and Policy Journal,* 2009 2(1):1–9; J. Kennedy and S. Morgan, "Cost- Related Prescription Nonadherence in the United States and Canada: A System-Level Comparison Using the 2007 International Health Policy Survey in Seven Countries," *Clinical Therapeutics,* Jan. 2009 31(1):213–19.

4. R. L. Kravitz, R. M. Epstein, M. D. Feldman et al., "Influence of Patients' Requests for Direct-to- Consumer Advertised Antidepressants: A Randomized Controlled Trial," *Journal of the American Medical Association,* April 27, 2005 293(16):1995–2002.

5. L. F. Berkman, "Social Epidemiology: Social Determinants of Health in the United States: Are We Losing Ground?" *Annual Review of Public Health,* April 29, 2009 30:27–41.

6. C. Schoen, S. R. Collins, J. L. Kriss, and M. M. Doty, "How Many Are Underinsured? Trends Among U.S. Adults, 2003 and 2007," *Health Affairs* Web Exclusive, June 10, 2008: w298–w309.

7. Descriptions of health care systems: Australia, Canada, Denmark, England, France, Germany, Italy, the Netherlands, New Zealand, Norway, Sweden, Switzerland, and the United States (New York: The Commonwealth Fund, forthcoming).

8. R. Tamblyn, R. Laprise, J. A. Hanley et al., "Adverse Events Associated with Prescription Drug Cost-Sharing Among Poor and Elderly Persons," *Journal of the American Medical Association,* Jan. 24–31, 2001 285(4):421–29; J. Hsu, M. Price, J.

Huang et al., "Unintended Consequences of Caps on Medicare Drug Benefits," *New England Journal of Medicine,* June 1, 2006 354(22):2349–59.

9. A. Austvoll-Dahlgren, M. Aaserud, G. Vist et al., "Pharmaceutical Policies: Effects of Cap and Copayment on Rational Drug Use," *Cochrane Database of Systematic Reviews: Reviews,* Jan. 23, 2008 1:CD007017; A. S. Adams, S. B. Soumerai, and D. Ross-Degnan, "The Case for a Medicare Drug Coverage Benefit: A Critical Review of the Empirical Evidence," *Annual Review of Public Health,* 2001 22:49–61; T. B. Gibson, R. J. Ozminkowski, and R. Z. Goetzel, "The Effects of Prescription Drug Cost Sharing: A Review of the Evidence," *American Journal of Managed Care,* Nov. 2005 11(11):730–40.

10. N. K. Choudhry, A. R. Patrick, E. M. Antman et al., "Cost-Effectiveness of Providing Full Drug Coverage to Increase Medication Adherence in Post-Myocardial Infarction Medicare Beneficiaries," *Circulation,* March 11, 2008 117(10):1261–68; S. Thompson and E. Mossialos, *Primary Care and Prescription Drugs: Coverage, Cost-Sharing, and Financial Protection in Six European Countries* (New York: The Commonwealth Fund, March 2010).

11. Morgan, Kennedy, Boothe et al., "Toward an Understanding of High Performance," 2009; S. Morgan, M. McMahon, C. Mitton et al., "Centralized Drug Review Processes in Australia, New Zealand, the United Kingdom, and Canada," *Health Affairs,* March/April 2006 25(2):337–47.

12. S. Morgan, M. McMahon, and C. Mitton, "Centralising Drug Review to Improve Coverage Decisions: Economic Lessons from (and for) Canada," *Applied Health Economics and Health Policy,* 2006 5(2):67–73; S. Morgan, K. Bassett, and B. Mintzes, "Outcomes-Based Drug Coverage in British Columbia," *Health Affairs,* May/June 2004 23(3):269–76.

13. C. Schoen, D. Helms, and A. Folsom, *Harnessing Health Care Markets for the Public Interest: Insights for U.S. Health Reform from the German and Dutch Multipayer Systems* (New York: The Commonwealth Fund, Dec. 2009).

14. What Will Happen Under Health Reform—And What's Next? The Commonwealth Fund, *Columbia Journalism Review, May 2010 supplement.*

15. J. Kennedy and S. Morgan, "Cost-Related Prescription Nonadherence in the United States and Canada: A System-Level Comparison Using the 2007 International Health Policy Survey in Seven Countries," *Clinical Therapeutics,* Jan. 2009 31(1):213–19; and J. Kennedy and S. Morgan, "A Cross-National Study of Prescription Nonadherance Due to Cost: Data from the Joint Canada –U.S. Survey of Health," *Clinical Therapeutics,* Aug. 2006 28(8):1217–24.

> *"Drug companies spend over 10 years and up to $2.6 billion bringing a drug to market. ... Even after accounting for their research investments, however, drug companies are among the most profitable public businesses in America."*

Nothing Stops Drug Companies from Charging the Highest Market Price

AARP

In the following viewpoint, the AARP addresses the fact that even though criticism is at its peak in terms of how expensive medications are, the costs continue to rise. The author reiterates that because there is such a demand for medications, consumers will pay whatever the price is to keep their health in good standing or survive, and because the US allows drug companies to essentially set their own prices, there's no positive end in sight right now for decreasing drug costs. While large drug companies will make it seem like they are reinvesting much of their profits into research and development, the pharmaceutical industry is still one of the most profitable industries in the country. AARP is a nonprofit organization focused on helping Americans over age fifty.

As you read, consider the following questions:

1. How much does Bavencio, a new cancer drug approved in March, cost per year per patient?
2. What percent do prescription drugs account for of the nation's health care costs?
3. How long does it take to bring a new drug to market?

For Susan Goodreds, Repatha has been as close as you can get to a miracle drug. The 74-year-old resident of Delray Beach, Fla., has a hereditary disorder that causes dangerously high cholesterol levels. Without medicine, her "bad" cholesterol count was in the 300s; statin drugs brought the count to about 220. With Repatha, it has fallen to 35.

The catch is, simply, cost. Repatha, a new medicine that made headlines in March when a large-scale study confirmed some of its beneficial effects, costs $14,000 annually, or nearly $1,200 for each month's injection. Even with insurance, Goodreds pays $4,650 a year for it. Add in other prescription drugs and medical costs, and her yearly health bill is $13,500—equal to most of her fixed income. "I'm faced with some hard decisions about whether to stay on the drug," Goodreds says. "I still have a lot of things I want to do with my life."

Confusion, anxiety and anger over the high cost of medicine has been on the rise for more than a decade. But even as the chorus of criticism has grown louder, the price of pharmaceutical products in the U.S. continues to skyrocket.

Consider:

- The cost of Bavencio, a new cancer drug approved in March, is about $156,000 a year per patient.
- A new muscular dystrophy drug came on the market late last year for an eye-popping price of $300,000 annually.
- In 2016, the FDA appproved Tecentriq, a new bladder cancer treatment that costs $12,500 a month, or $150,000 a year.

- Even older drugs that have long been on the market are not immune: The cost of insulin tripled between 2002 and 2013, despite no notable changes in the formulation or manufacturing process. And the four-decade-old EpiPen, a lifesaving allergy medication, has seen a price hike of 500 percent since 2007. Public outrage this past winter over its price tag ($609 for a package of two injectors) helped to speed up the arrival of lower-cost generic variations to the market.

The issue of high drug prices came up frequently in the recent election cycle, and in a speech in Kentucky in March, President Trump called drug prices "outrageous." Increasingly, Americans are asking the same question of pharmaceutical companies: Why?

The Ways of Drug Pricing

"The simple answer is because there's nothing stopping them," says Leigh Purvis, director of health services research for the AARP Public Policy Institute.

Other countries drive a much harder bargain with drug companies. In contrast, the U.S. allows drug companies to pretty much set their own prices.

And as we all know, when demand is high for a product, companies often raise prices. That's exactly the case for many prescription drugs.

Tens of millions of Americans suffer from conditions like high cholesterol, high blood pressure and diabetes, all of which can be treated successfully with prescription medications.

More recently, drugmakers have developed game-changing therapies for a host of serious illnesses, including multiple sclerosis, hepatitis C and several cancers. That means people are living longer lives.

The supply of a newer medicine, however, is controlled entirely by the drug manufacturer that holds the patent rights. That gives the manufacturer a monopoly on the drug for the 20-year life of the patent. During that time, it is free to raise the price as frequently and as much as the market will bear. An example: Last February, the price of Evzio, an auto-injected drug that is used to treat opioid overdose, jumped to over $4,000—from just $690 in 2014—just as demand for the medicine was quickly rising.

You may not realize the high cost of medicine if you're relatively healthy and have insurance to cover those occasional needs for, say, a week's course of antibiotics. But if you or someone in your family develops a chronic or serious condition, prepare for sticker shock—even if you have insurance.

When Janet Huston was diagnosed with a rare stomach cancer in 2009, surgery seemed to offer a cure. But a year later the cancer—called gastrointestinal stromal tumor or GIST—returned with a vengeance. The 66-year-old retired lawyer is now taking an arsenal of drugs, including Gleevec, to contain her tumor and control its symptoms. But the medicines that allow her to lead "a somewhat normal life" cost her more than $17,000 a year, including about $12,000 for Gleevec.

"That's about 30 percent of my total income," says Huston, who lives in Des Moines, Iowa, on Social Security and a modest pension from her years as an attorney. "I don't always take my medication as I should, especially in the months when income taxes and property taxes come due," she admits.

It's not just people like Huston who suffer financially. "High prescription drug prices affect everyone," Purvis says. "Even if patients are fortunate enough to have good health care coverage, higher prices translate into higher out-of-pocket costs, premiums and deductibles. And greater spending by taxpayer-funded programs like Medicare and Medicaid are eventually passed along to all Americans in the form of higher taxes, cuts to public programs or both."

Put even more simply: One reason that your health insurance rates are high is because you are subsidizing other people's high-cost medicines. For example, imagine the euphoria if a company developed a breakthrough treatment for Alzheimer's disease. Let's say it costs $60,000 a year per patient, and it gets prescribed to every American with the disease. To pay for the medicine, insurance premiums for each privately insured person in the U.S. would increase by more than $140 per month, based on a new calculator developed by the Biotechnology Innovation Organization.

A Contorted Marketplace

If you needed a new TV, you would do some research, shop around and pick the best model at the price you can afford. That creates competition that pushes prices down. The market for prescription drugs doesn't work that way. For example, you don't make the product choice—your health care provider does. And doctors and nurse practitioners often do so in the dark: There's little information available to compare one drug to another. The Food and Drug Administration (FDA) does not require drug companies to prove that their new products are better than existing products. So many physicians write prescriptions for the drugs they're most familiar with—and that information often comes from manufacturers themselves. Drug companies spend $24 billion a year marketing to health care professionals.

Other factors that cause the drug market to be skewed include:

Patent law

Pharmaceutical companies have become adept at coming up with strategies to extend their monopoly on a drug beyond the expiration of its original patent. For example, they can seek approval for a "new" product that is a slight variation on the original, such as extended release formulations, or by creating therapies that combine two existing drugs into one pill. "The longer that a drug company is able to maintain its monopoly, the longer it can continue to charge whatever it wants for its product," Purvis says.

Limits on Medicare

One of the largest purchasers of prescription drugs, Medicare is blocked by law from negotiating prices. When Congress was debating the law that created Medicare Part D (which took effect in 2006), lobbyists from the pharmaceutical industry convinced legislators that giving Medicare negotiating power would amount to price control.

Compare Medicare with the Veterans Health Administration (VHA), the part of the Department of Veterans Affairs that handles medical care. The VHA does have the ability to negotiate drug prices. As a result, it pays 80 percent less for brand name drugs than Medicare Part D pays, according to a 2015 report by Carleton University in Ottawa, Ontario, and Public Citizen, a public advocacy group. The VHA gets its negotiating power from its formulary, a list of prescription drugs that it will cover. Medicare and Medicaid, by contrast, are required to cover almost all drugs approved by the FDA, regardless of whether a cheaper, equally effective drug is available.

Multiple middlemen

When you pick up a drug at the pharmacy, you often don't know what its real price is—that is established between the manufacturer and your insurer. You just pay the agreed-upon copay rate. Today, insurance companies rarely negotiate prices directly with drug manufacturers. Instead, most insurers work with pharmacy benefit managers, who negotiate rebates and discounts on the company's behalf—often in exchange for preferential placement on their list of covered medicines. Pharmacy benefit managers add yet another participant to what is already a complex system.

The R&D Explanation

The pharmaceutical industry offers several responses to the charges of excessively high prices. First, it notes that prescription drugs account for just 10 percent of the nation's health care costs; by comparison, 32 percent of costs go to hospital care, according to a 2016 report from Medicare.

It also notes that an open market means that "patients in the U.S. can access the most innovative treatments far earlier than any other country," says Robert Zirkelbach, executive vice president at the Pharmaceutical Research and Manufacturers of America (PhRMA), the industry trade group. For example, data from PhRMA show that patients in Europe wait an average of nearly two years longer to get access to cancer medicines than American patients.

But the industry's primary defense of rising medicine prices are the high costs associated with drug development.

Drug companies spend over 10 years and up to $2.6 billion bringing a drug to market, according to a 2016 Journal of Health Economics article based on research by the Tufts Center for the Study of Drug Development (which gets a minority of its operating funds from the pharmaceutical industry). Of that amount, $1.4 billion is actual costs—items like salaries, labs, clinical-trial expenses and manufacturing. The remaining $1.2 billion is "capital costs": what the company sacrifices by investing time and money in an unproven drug. Some experts dispute these numbers, saying they overstate the true costs.

Even after accounting for their research investments, however, drug companies are among the most profitable public businesses in America. And an analysis from the research company Global Data revealed that 9 out of 10 big pharmaceutical companies spend more on marketing than on research. Most of them also have big budgets for lobbyists to ensure the laws continue to work in their favor. The Center for Responsive Politics puts the number of pharmaceutical industry lobbyists at 804 in 2016.

Further, some drug companies are moving away from doing all of their research in-house and instead are buying smaller companies with promising products. About 70 percent of industry sales come from drugs that originated in small companies, up from 30 percent in 1990, according to a Boston Consulting Group survey.

In addition, drug companies increasingly focus on products that can generate the highest profits. The majority of drugs approved by the FDA are now expensive specialty drugs. Many drug companies are also pursuing "orphan drugs"—medicines targeting diseases that afflict fewer than 200,000 people. These medications cost an average of $140,000 a year. The catch: Many orphan drugs eventually receive additional approvals as a treatment for other conditions, dramatically increasing the market for the drug.

The government supports orphan drug development with tax breaks and other incentives. In 2016, the pharmaceutical industry netted $1.76 billion in orphan drug tax credits.

Meanwhile, just five of the top 50 drug companies are spending money on much-needed new antibiotics—largely because these drugs aren't lucrative, the AARP Bulletin reported in November 2016. "In most cases, people only need to take an antibiotic for a couple of weeks to get rid of an infection. Compare that to medications for chronic conditions—which people go on taking every day for years—and you can understand why drugmakers aren't particularly interested," says Erik Gordon, a professor at the University of Michigan Ross School of Business.

There is nothing illegal with any of this: As publicly owned corporations, pharmaceutical firms focus on their bottom line. "Pharmaceutical executives say they have to be more aggressive to satisfy Wall Street," says John Rother, executive director of the Campaign for Sustainable Rx Pricing.

But there's evidence that drug companies will respond if pressured to lower prices. One example is patient-assistance programs. Kristin Agar, a 65-year-old clinical social worker in Little Rock, Ark., was diagnosed with lupus in 2009. Her doctor prescribed Benlysta, the only medication specifically approved for lupus. Her insurer would pay 80 percent, about $2,500 per infusion, but Agar had to pay the remaining $450 per dose.

"I couldn't afford that," says the self-employed professional. But when she applied for assistance, she was told she made too much money. "That just infuriated me," she says. Agar appealed the decision—and got her copay covered by the drugmaker for two years.

But a consensus is building that more must occur. "People are concerned about drug prices; more are being forced to make trade-offs between paying for their drugs and for food or rent," says AARP's Purvis. "The trends that we're seeing are simply unsustainable."

| "Patients' insulation from costs makes them less sensitive to all medical prices, and this lack of sensitivity encourages companies to charge higher prices."

Encouraging Competition Is the Answer to Affordable Pharmaceuticals

Charles L. Hooper and David R. Henderson

In the following viewpoint, Charles L. Hooper and David R. Henderson argue that we should stop looking at the pharmaceutical industry in terms of ethics. The authors contend that consumers' expectations of health care costs are skewed because insurance and copays insulate them from the real costs involved. The real solution, they say, is for the government and consumers to encourage healthy competition within the pharmaceutical industry. Once the free market takes over, prices will be driven down and the supply of medicine will increase. Hooper is president of Objective Insights, a consultancy for pharmaceutical and biotech companies. Henderson is professor of economics at the Naval Postgraduate school and a research fellow with the Hoover Institution.

"Want Cheaper Drugs?" by Charles L. Hooper and David R. Henderson, Cato Institute, 2016. Reprinted by permission.

As you read, consider the following questions:

1. What is the estimated cost behind adding one new drug to the market?
2. Why do Americans pay more for their drugs?
3. How would approval of more OTC drugs be a remedy for lower drug costs?

U.S. drug pricing is in the crosshairs. Martin Shkreli, formerly of Turing pharmaceuticals and KaloBios, made headlines last fall after he hiked the price for the 1950s-era drug Daraprim (pyrimethamine) nearly 5,500 percent. Throw in some supersized price increases by Valeant pharmaceuticals, condemnations by presidential candidates Hillary Clinton, Bernie Sanders, and Donald Trump, *Wall Street Journal* articles about high American drug prices, U.S. Senate and House committee hearings on drug pricing, and a comprehensive report on government spending on prescription drugs that is being prepared by the U.S. Department of Health and Human Services, and we have one pharmaceutical industry–sized black eye.

Every imaginable product and service has a price, and yet there is something different about pricing prescription medicines. The unique characteristics of this industry should be understood, lest politicians—eager to be seen addressing a "crisis"—severely damage an industry that has restored health and eased pain for hundreds of millions of Americans. To " x" drug pricing, we need more competition, more cost sharing, and the liberalization of some regulations.

Odd Market

Medicines prevent and cure debilitating and deadly diseases, and people place a high value on health. That's one reason drugs are expensive. But there are more reasons. Physicians prescribe drugs, but they don't personally pay—and often don't know—the prices of drugs. Pharmacists know the prices, but don't have much control over the prescribing decision. Patients are the primary beneficiaries of prescription drugs, but they pay only 22 percent of the cost, typically through their copays. And notice our use of the word "copays." Insured patients typically pay a fixed dollar amount—a copay—rather than a percentage of the drug's price, so for a drug with a copay of $20, patients do not have an incentive to care whether the drug is priced at $100 or $500. Third-party payers, both commercial and governmental, pay most of the cost, but they generally use a broad brush to put prescription drugs into copayment categories and apply restrictions. The result of all this is relatively muted demand-side pressure for lower drug prices.

Patients are heavily insulated from the costs of their care partly because of long-term efforts by policymakers and advocates on the political left. The Affordable Care Act was a notable exception to this trend and, according to the Kaiser Family Foundation, following the legislation's passage, patients' insurance deductibles have increased six times as fast as average wages. Presidential aspirant Hillary Clinton would insulate those patients more; her "solution" to the current drug price problem is to limit consumers' monthly out-of-pocket costs for medications. This would counteract one desired effect of the Affordable Care Act—encouraging drug consumers to economize—and would ultimately lead to higher drug prices. Patients' insulation from costs makes them less sensitive to all medical prices, and this lack of sensitivity encourages companies to charge higher prices. If patients paid a larger share of prices (or even knew the prices), then health care costs—including drug prices—would increase more slowly or even fall.

FDA Testing

The U.S. Food and Drug Administration contributes to high drug prices. Its costly approval process makes it hard for new drugs to reach the market, which keeps price competition between drug makers to a minimum. Economists Joseph DiMasi, Henry Grabowski, and Ronald Hansen at the Tufts Center for the Study of Drug Development have estimated that the costs behind adding one new drug to the market total nearly $2.6 billion. Why so high? Because so much of R&D is spent on drugs that fail along the way. This figure accounts for those "dry holes." DiMasi et al. estimate these costs have increased at 7 percent per year in real terms: $179 million in the 1970s, $413 million in the 1980s, $1 billion in the 1990s through early 2000s, and now $2.6 billion. if this 7 percent annual growth rate persists, costs can be expected to double every 10 years.

This imposing cost means that far fewer drugs are discovered, developed, and marketed, which means less competition, less overall pricing pressures, and higher drug prices. This is quite apparent to drug pricers. The ninth statin drug to enter a market competes against the previous eight, perhaps with improved efficacy and a similar price, or perhaps with similar efficacy and a lower price. Competition in that market keeps prices down because customers have good alternatives. The first and only drug for a particular type of cancer, conversely, competes only with whatever archaic and ineffective therapies were used previously; competition is minimal and prices can be higher.

But wouldn't clinical trials still be needed absent FDA regulation, in order for the drug to earn consumer acceptance? They usually would. But even if doctors and patients would always be as cautious about new drugs as the FDA is, there would likely be more effcient ways of getting the same information about a drug's safety and efficacy. For example, the FDA required Roxro Pharma to run clinical trials for its Sprix (intranasal ketorolac tromethamine) nasal spray, a non-steroidal anti-inflammatory drug. That might have been reasonable had the active ingredient in Sprix not had two decades of real-world experience. It was clear that ketorolac worked; the only remaining questions were specific to the intranasal delivery system. What the FDA required for approval made no sense but cost millions of dollars and took two years. Moreover, doctors and patients show by their behavior with off-label uses that they are willing to consume drugs that have not been tested specifically, or approved by the FDA, for those uses.

Foreign Markets

It's often noted that drugs are much cheaper in other countries that have more socialized health care systems. While that is true, the disparity isn't quite as large as is claimed; for instance, U.S. consumers make much greater use of generic drugs, and generics are cheaper here than in Canada or Europe. Still, there is a significant price difference.

There are three principle reasons for this difference. First, most people around the world are poorer than Americans. Pricing based on value—economists call this "market segmentation" or "price discrimination"—means setting lower prices where incomes are lower. A Wharton Business School analysis showed that price differences across countries were somewhat consistent with per-capita income differences. In some cases, people are so poor that drug companies simply provide the medicines for free.

Second, most governments negotiate drug prices. While some may cheer this, it involves the exercise of monopsony power—market power on the buyer's side. These governments are saying, in effect, that under normal circumstances, if they can't buy a drug cheaply, their citizens won't get it. As a result, their populations do without some breakthrough medicines.

Drug companies would likely extend price discrimination to poorer Americans if not for a perverse incentive in the nation's Medicaid program. Medicaid requires drug companies to charge it the lowest domestic price offered on every drug. That unintentionally dissuades drug companies from offering lower prices to low-income Americans who aren't enrolled in Medicaid. Those same low prices would then have to be offered to the huge Medicaid program and the smaller 340B program, lowering overall company profits. It is wrong to prevent drug companies from making mutually agreeable deals with these patients.

The third reason branded drugs are cheaper in other countries is that some governments threaten to invalidate a drug's patents if the (typically foreign) drug maker charges a price that government officials deem "too high." Thus, so-called compulsory licensing is really just a violation of intellectual property rights. When faced with a choice between making no money or some money, most drug companies choose the latter. That outcome does not legitimize the process.

The result is that Americans subsidize global drug research and development costs because Europeans and Canadians pay so little for drugs. in essence, new drugs are developed for the U.S. market, with its large, wealthy population and generally less-regulated drug pricing. Many breakthrough drugs would never have been developed given, say, English pricing levels. Once drugs are developed for the American market, other countries effectively hitch a free—or at least cheap—ride, relying on Americans to subsidize the R&D costs. The problem is, if we Americans also try to free ride, there may not be many new rides.

Pushing Prices Down

Once a drug is approved, the $2.6 billion development and approval cost is "sunk." A clear-thinking company will ignore it when setting a price based on what the market will bear; the company need only recover manufacturing, marketing, and distribution costs in order to make production of the already-invented drug financially worthwhile. But at some point, all companies need to consider a price high enough to make the whole venture profitable from the outset; the sunk costs were not always sunk and must be paid somehow. Otherwise, why would drug companies embark on a money-losing venture?

How much lower would drug prices be if not for the FDA's mandated approval costs and the subsequent damping of competition? We don't know, but some analysts have suggested a full order of magnitude less, based on observations of markets with lots of competition and those with little. Occasionally we do get to see particular drugs that enter a market where similar drugs were marketed without FDA approval. The new drugs, which received FDA approval and marketing exclusivity, are always priced much higher. One such drug, Makena, which helps prevent premature births, was priced at 100 times the price of existing non-approved drugs for the same purpose.

The reason that drug companies even consider large price increases for their products is a perception that their drugs are currently underpriced relative to their value. In 2003, Abbott Laboratories raised the price of Norvir, an HIV drug introduced in 1996, from $54 to $265 a month. Abbott received widespread criticism for the decision, partly as a result of internal memos that exposed the decision as a tactic to help another Abbott HIV drug, Kaletra, which is a combination of Norvir and another drug. As offensive as the price increase was to some, Abbott believed that the price of Norvir was far below its value. The protease inhibitor had serious side effects that prevented its stand-alone use. However, Abbott had discovered that in small doses, Norvir boosted the effectiveness of other protease inhibitors; it soon enjoyed widespread use as a component in the drug cocktails taken by AIDS patients. On its own, Norvir has a low value; in combinations with other drugs, it has a high value.

With little holding them back, why don't manufacturers of drugs facing minimal competition set outlandish prices like $1 million per dose? The simple answer is they can't; even monopolies are bounded by what consumers are willing and able to spend. Preventing pre-term births, curing hepatitis C, treating HIV, limiting the effects of Parkinson's disease, and giving cancer patients another year to live are truly valuable outcomes, but the economic value is still capped and must meet the implicit approval of health plans, physicians, and patients. After all, if any of the three balk, the sale is lost. So at least two market mechanisms limit drug prices.

Two other remedies that the federal government could use to keep pharmaceutical costs down are the approval of more over-the-counter (OTC) drugs and allowing drug reimportation.

OTC status can lead to strong price competition. For instance, OTC proton pump inhibitors and H2 antagonists are priced at about 10 percent of the prices of their prescription versions.

Why would OTC drugs be so much cheaper? Patients who pay 100 percent of the cost—as they do with OTC drugs—are far more price sensitive, and companies price accordingly.

Drug reimportation—allowing patients to import drugs that have been sold in other countries—would circumvent both the FDA's high-cost approval process and Medicaid's "best price" requirement. The only requirement is that these sales should be voluntary for all parties; U.S. drug makers should not be coerced to sell to foreign countries that then sell the drugs back into U.S. markets. Some have argued that these "re-imports" should not be allowed because the drugs are sold to wholesalers on the condition that they not be sold back to buyers in the United States. If this is the contractual arrangement with foreign wholesalers, then they certainly are breaching their contract, and that shouldn't be allowed. But enforcing contracts is not the job of U.S. Customs, the FDA, or the Department of Health and Human Services.

Conclusion

It should be noted that misbehaving drug companies like Turing and Valeant have been punished heavily for their dramatic price increases. Valeant lost 70 percent of its market share by November 2015 and Turing posted a $15 million third-quarter loss. (And Shkreli, it should be added, was arrested for securities fraud.) A generic competitor announced that it would begin selling a version of Daraprim for 0.1 percent of Turing's price. Already facing lawsuits and government investigations, these companies have been ostracized by the rest of the pharmaceutical industry; the industry organization, BIO, even took the unusual step of expelling Turing.

Those developments underscore that the best long-term solution for keeping a lid on drug prices is good old-fashioned competition from more new drug approvals and more prescription-to-OTC approvals, combined with cost sharing and the elimination of the Medicaid "best price" regulation. Cost sharing gives patients an incentive to use medicines only when the benefits are greater than their share of the drug's price, which will put further downward pressure on prices. Not only will further competition hold down prices, but also the concomitant increased supply of good medicines will help Americans live better and longer lives.

Outrage over drug prices may someday be a historical curiosity. Until then, the industry will face periodic black eyes and politicians who, through the unintended consequences of their actions, may make matters worse. The best solution isn't one of clamping down on industry, but of relaxing some rules and unleashing a flood of new therapies.

> *"Overall, Americans use more medicines than people in other developed countries. They rank first for their use of antipsychotics as well as drugs for dementia, respiratory problems and rheumatoid arthritis."*

Prescription Demand Is Why Americans Pay So Much For Drugs

Valerie Paris

In the following viewpoint, Valerie Paris argues that Americans spend much more on pharmaceuticals than most other countries around the world. Plain and simple, Americans use more medications than those who dwell in other developed countries, and because the US has some of the highest prescription drug costs in the world, it makes complete sense why Americans spend so much money on pharmaceuticals. Paris argues that there doesn't appear to be an end in sight in terms of drug costs falling, or the amount of prescriptions that Americans need, so we can expect that trend to continue. Paris is an economist who works on the analysis of health systems for the Organisation for Economic Cooperation and Development (OECD).

As you read, consider the following questions:

1. How much does the United States spends per person per year on pharmaceuticals?
2. Generics now account for what percentage of pharmaceutical spending?
3. Prices in the US for brand-name patented drugs are how many times as high as in the United Kingdom or Australia?

The United States spends almost $1,000 per person per year on pharmaceuticals. That's around 40 percent more than the next highest spender, Canada, and more than twice as much as than countries like France and Germany spend. So why does the U.S. spend so much? Is it because Americans take more medicines or because they pay higher prices? Can Americans afford the drugs they need? And will the Affordable Care Act change anything?

Americans Use More Pharmaceuticals

Overall, Americans use more medicines than people in other developed countries. They rank first for their use of antipsychotics as well as drugs for dementia, respiratory problems and rheumatoid arthritis. This is partly explained by medical needs: The burden of disease in the U.S. — as measured in "years of life lost" — is higher than in many OECD countries for the most common forms of heart disease, chronic obstructive pulmonary diseases, diabetes, and Alzheimer's. Several factors may explain this, including high levels of obesity and high rates of diagnosis.

Americans also have faster access to new drugs than patients in many other countries. That's in part because the U.S. has always been a very attractive market for pharmaceutical companies: It's big, accounting for 34 percent of the world market; has low levels of price regulation; and offers few barriers to market entry once FDA approval has been secured. (By contrast, in some other countries

THE PUBLIC'S NUMBER 1 PRIORITY

The emerging issue in health care is drug costs — despite the fact that most people say they can afford their drugs and greatly value the role drugs can play in making their lives better. One likely reason this is the case: Drug costs are the first thing people think of when they think of the growing out of pocket costs they are paying for health care, at a time when their wages have been relatively flat.

In our Kaiser Family Foundation polling in April, surprisingly, "making sure that high-cost drugs for chronic conditions are affordable to those who need them" emerged as the public's No. 1 priority for President Barack Obama and Congress, with 75% of the public saying it should be a top priority, far ahead of various other Affordable Care Act issues. "Government action to lower drug prices" was No. 2, picked by 60 % of the public and by 51% of republicans. (Respondents could choose multiple top priorities.)

Then, in our August polling, we asked which health costs people with health coverage find to be the greatest burden. As the chart below shows, deductibles led a closely bunched list, followed by premium payments, drug costs and doctor visits. Deductibles have been rising steadily each year, especially for people who work for smaller employers, as insurance has gradually been moving from more to less comprehensive, with more "skin in the game" for consumers.

You might think people prioritized action on prescription drugs in our poll because they have been hearing about high drug costs in the news. But that doesn't appear to be the case, with only 5% of the public reporting that they followed stories about expensive treatments for hepatitis C very closely and 6% saying the same about new cholesterol drugs. Instead, personal experience seems to be driving people's impressions. Over half of the public reports taking a prescription drug, and almost 40% of those people report taking four or more drugs.

"Why Higher Drug Costs Are Consumers' Biggest Cost Worry," by Drew Altman, The Wall Street Journal, September 8, 2015.

there may be a time lag between clinical approval of a drug and the point when it is added to official lists of reimbursable drugs.)

The result is that companies often choose the U.S. to launch new products. And, because the US market is so big and profitable, investments in research and development have long been steered towards meeting its clinical needs.

Drug Costs are High in the U.S.

But if Americans take more pharmaceuticals, they also pay more for them. Prices in the U.S. for brand-name patented drugs are 50 to 60 percent higher than in France and twice as high as in the United Kingdom or Australia. That's because in many countries, government agencies essentially regulate the prices of medicines and set limits to the amount they will reimburse; they may only agree to pay for a drug if they feel that the price is justified by the therapeutic benefits. This centralized approach can also give them more bargaining power over drug makers.

By contrast, in the U.S. insurers typically accept the price set by the makers for each drug, especially when there is no competition in a therapeutic area, and then cover the cost with high copayments. Where there are competing drugs, insurers enjoy more bargaining power and may negotiate discounts with manufacturers in exchange for lower cost-sharing for patients. In off-patent markets, the competition is fierce and prices of generic drugs are low. Generic penetration is high in the U.S. and their use spreads quickly: within six months of a patent expiring on a drug, generics typically account for 80 percent of the market. Generics now account for 28 percent of pharmaceutical spending and 84 percent of drugs dispensed in the U.S., which is high by OECD standards.

Many Americans Can't Afford Their Medications

Can patients access the drugs they need? While the financial burden for households has declined over the past years, it is clear that many Americans are not taking their recommended medications because of the high costs. A recent survey showed that around one in five U.S. adults did not fill out their prescription or skipped doses because of the costs of medicines in 2013. The proportion was less than one in ten in Germany, Canada and Australia. The difference is that, unlike in the U.S., health coverage in most other OECD tends to be universal. Patients often have to share the costs of pharmaceutical treatments, but they get exemptions if they are poor, severely ill or have reached a certain level of out-of-pocket payments.

What will change with the Affordable Care Act?

The Affordable Care Act has already reduced copayments for Medicare patients and it will increase the number of people covered for prescription drugs. By making drugs more affordable, the reform will likely increase the volume of drugs used in the U.S. — prescription rates are likely to rise, as will patients' compliance to treatments.

But will prices fall? The reform does not provide new leverage to lower prices and nor does it remove barriers to price negotiation for some Medicare plans. At best, insurers may use comparative effectiveness studies from the Patient-Centered Outcomes Research Institute to encourage more appropriate treatments. But without further change, the prices of new and highly specialized drugs will likely rise, especially at a time when pharmaceutical firms are facing sluggish revenue prospects.

Will this, in turn, mean that the U.S. spends more on drugs? It's true that in the U.S., as in many wealthy OECD countries, pharmaceutical spending has been declining in real terms. For some countries, this trend is explained by cuts in government spending in the wake of the Great Recession. In the U.S., much of this decline is explained by the fact that patents on a number of top drugs have expired, meaning they can be replaced by cheaper generics. This effect is expected to last another two or three years; after that, future trends in spending are harder to predict.

Periodical and Internet Sources Bibliography

*The following articles have been selected to supplement the diverse
views presented in this chapter.*

Julie Appleby, "New hepatitis C drugs' price prompts an ethical
   debate: Who deserves to get them?," The Washington Post, May 2,
   2014. https://www.washingtonpost.com/business/new-hepatitis-
   c-drugs-price-prompts-an-ethical-debate-who-deserves-to-get-
   them/2014/05/01/73582abc-cfac-11e3-937f-d3026234b51c_story.
   html?utm_term=.f1b03fd41ff3.

Raquel Baldelomar, "Where Is The Line Between Ethical And
   Legal?," Forbes, July 21, 2016. https://www.forbes.com/sites/
   raquelbaldelomar/2016/07/21/where-is-the-line-between-what-
   is-ethical-and-legal/#1bca95f1250b.

Stacy Cowley, "Doctors blast ethics of $100,000 cancer drugs,"
   CNN, April 26, 2013. http://money.cnn.com/2013/04/25/news/
   economy/cancer-drug-cost/index.html.

Frank David, "Pharma CEOs Should Take A Stand On Egregious
   Price Increase -- But They Won't," Forbes, September 20, 2015.
   https://www.forbes.com/sites/frankdavid/2015/09/20/why-
   pharma-companies-should-take-a-stand-on-turings-drug-
   pricing-and-why-they-probably-wont/#bde5a85f90b5.

Carolyn Johnson, "Here's why pharma is happy to help foot the bill
   for this $750,000 drug," The Washington Post, June 9, 2017.
   https://www.washingtonpost.com/business/heres-why-pharma-
   is-happy-to-help-foot-the-bill-for-this-750000-drug/2017/06/09/
   f29da05a-4a14-11e7-9669-250d0b15f83b_story.html?utm_
   term=.a1125baca8fe.

Scott Knoer, "How to Stop Immoral Drug Price Increases," Time,
   September 7, 2016. http://time.com/4475970/stop-immoral-
   drug-prices.

Daniel Kozarich, "Mylan's EpiPen Pricing Crossed Ethical
   Boundaries," Fortune, September 27, 2016. http://fortune.
   com/2016/09/27/mylan-epipen-heather-bresch.

John LaMattina, "Pharma's Reputation Continues to Suffer—What
   Can Be Done To Fix It?," Forbes, January 18, 2013. https://www

.forbes.com/sites/johnlamattina/2013/01/18/pharmas-reputation-continues-to-suffer-what-can-be-done-to-fix-it/#60684df82aa5.

Katie Thomas, "The Complex Math Behind Spiraling Prescription Drug Prices," The New York Times, August 24, 2016. https://www.nytimes.com/2016/08/25/business/high-drug-prices-explained-epipen-heart-medications.html.

Jim Zarroli, "Turing Pharmaceuticals Retreats From Plan To Raise Price Of Daraprim," NPR, September 23, 2015. http://www.npr.org/2015/09/23/442907028/turing-pharmaceuticals-retreats-from-plan-to-raise-price-of-daraprim.

CHAPTER 4

Will We See Legislative Changes to the Way Drugs Are Priced?

Chapter Preface

Action and change are requested of the government by the people daily, for everything from the way police are trained to the legalization of marijuana, but one of the most consistent requests from the people is for the government to step in and make changes to the ways that prescription drugs are priced in America. Coincidentally enough, the party that is supposed to govern and control drug pricing is actually the same one that is allowing drug prices to continue to soar. Throughout this chapter, one of the viewpoints that readers will analyze is that of the relationship between large pharmaceutical companies and politicians, and all of the funding that politicians receive on the campaign trail from big pharmaceutical companies. Readers will also be taken through a viewpoint that points the finger at the government, stating that it is US government policies that are keeping prescription drug costs high.

Opposing viewpoints in this chapter present positive findings on government action in the battle against high drug costs. One of those viewpoints comes from a physician who defends the government, reminding readers that it is ultimately the government who is able to negotiate prices down with drug manufacturers, which is something that private purchasers typically are not able to do as well. Another viewpoint highlights transparency bills that have been attempted by certain politicians over the year, which would make it mandatory for pharmaceutical companies to disclose spending information, thus helping to set a market value for the drug, in hopes of lowering costs. Each side is well-represented in chapter 4.

This concluding chapter displays the landscape of the government's role in controlling—or contributing—to high drug prices, but more importantly, it gets readers thinking about the future and what it holds for big pharma manufacturers and consumers' wallets down the road.

> *"Policymaking around drug prices is politically difficult. Strong pharmaceutical interest groups oppose seemingly any action in this space, arguing that even actions targeted at generic drugs would decrease innovator companies' incentives to invest in new cures."*

Government Reforms Can Address Consumer Concerns

Rachel Sachs

In the following viewpoint, Rachel Sachs argues that the government can initiate reforms that would lower drug prices. Although the author admits that policymaking is extremely challenging when it comes to pharmaceuticals, she outlines several possible ways reforms could take place, both on the state and federal level. One suggestion is the enactment of transparency laws, which would make details about the various costs involved in pricing drugs available to consumers. The author also notes that the private sector is working to curb drug costs, but that government action could be faster and more effective. Sachs is a graduate of Harvard Law School and is associate professor of law at Washington University in St. Louis, Missouri.

As you read, consider the following questions:

1. What percentage of Kaiser Permanente's respondents indicated that lowering drug prices should be a top priority for the US government?
2. What is the current price of the EpiPen, according to the viewpoint?
3. Which US state was the first to enact a transparency law?

Martin Shkreli. Valeant Pharmaceuticals. Mylan. These names have become big news, but just a year ago, most Americans devoted little time and attention to the question of pharmaceutical pricing. Now, a Kaiser Health Tracking Poll released Oct. 27 suggests many people care more about the increasing prices of drugs than they do about any other aspect of health care reform.

Nearly three in four, or 74 percent of respondents, said that making sure that high-cost drugs for chronic conditions are affordable for patients should be a top priority for the next president and Congress. And 63 percent similarly said that government action to lower prescription drug prices should be a top priority.

This poll comes on the heels of highly publicized scandals involving individuals and companies who hike the prices of products like the EpiPen, a life-saving anaphylaxis treatment whose price roughly quintupled in five years, to more than US$600, or Daraprim, a drug used to treat parasitic infections whose price increased by 5,000 percent overnight.

Many drug makers and their CEOs have raised the prices of their products with impunity. As prices have risen, so has the level of outrage among consumers. Policymakers are taking note.

Importantly, to the extent that high drug prices are a problem, it is not an easy one to solve. As academics have argued, there are many different reasons why a drug may have a high price.

We simultaneously want to reward companies who come up with new, innovative cures for chronic conditions while preventing companies from raising the price of older generic drugs without good reason. Coming up with policy interventions that would target only the latter activity while at the same time providing certainty of profit potential to innovators up front can be challenging.

At the same time, policymaking around drug prices is politically difficult. Strong pharmaceutical interest groups oppose seemingly any action in this space, arguing that even actions targeted at generic drugs would decrease innovator companies' incentives to invest in new cures. Although I and others have argued that this concern is oversimplified, it nonetheless has had a significant impact on the debate.

Despite this opposition, the growing appetite among the public for doing something, anything, about high drug prices has led to a proliferation of policy proposals on the subject. These proposals would affect different drugs and would act on different institutions within the drug pricing ecosystem. As we approach Election Day, it is worth thinking about which of these actions would be implemented at different levels of government. Given the different proposals and the concerns that people have expressed over high drug prices, it's worth looking at possible solutions.

Reforms at the Federal Level

Many of the most commonly discussed reforms would take place at the federal level. Although there are greater political challenges to enacting change at the federal level, the potential effects are also much broader than for reforms enacted at the state level.

Allowing Medicare to Negotiate Drug Prices

The most commonly proposed drug pricing reform would give Medicare the authority to negotiate drug prices. The thinking is that because Medicare has such purchasing power, it will be able to demand discounts for the tens of millions of Americans covered by its plans. This solution is so popular that it has been praised by both Secretary Clinton and Donald Trump. And yet, it wouldn't work on its own.

Here's the problem: Not only is Medicare itself legally prohibited from negotiating drug prices, but it is also legally required to cover certain prescription drugs. Medicare can't get up and walk away from the bargaining table if it doesn't like the price the pharmaceutical company is offering, which significantly limits its ability to demand discounts from companies.

If Medicare were given the authority to decline to cover a drug if its manufacturer did not provide a discount, that would improve its bargaining power – but that would also prevent Medicare beneficiaries from accessing the drug in question, which is highly unpopular. Although some scholars have proposed creative ways around this problem, none has yet made it into the political discussion.

Constrain Price Increases

Much of the public outrage accompanying high drug prices has come in response to companies that raise the prices of old drugs, seemingly only to increase their profits. As such, a number of proposals would constrain the ability of drug companies to increase their prices over time. In fact, one of these even became law in the wake of Martin Shkreli's activities around Daraprim, enabling Medicaid to recoup additional rebates on a generic drug if its price rose faster than inflation.

Recently, Secretary Clinton has put forth a plan that would prevent such price hikes more broadly, outside of just the Medicaid program. At the same time, Secretary Clinton's proposal would account for the reasons behind the price increase, allowing increases where they're needed to address situations like manufacturing problems. Because this proposal is limited to older drugs, it may face less political opposition, although its passage will surely not be easy.

Reforms at the State Level

The federal government is not the only entity interested in curbing high drug prices. Many states are currently considering other measures that would take effect only within their borders, although some might have follow-on effects more broadly.

State Drug Price Cap Laws

California and Ohio are currently considering ballot initiatives to cap what drug manufacturers can charge to public payers in the state (such as Medicaid) at the price the VA pays for them.

Because these initiatives don't distinguish between different kinds of drugs, affecting both new, highly effective products as well as older or more marginal ones, we should carefully consider their real-world impact, and there are persuasive arguments on either side. My bigger concern, however, is that these initiatives would not actually work to accomplish their stated purpose.

Not only are the prices the VA pays often confidential, but as with Medicare, state Medicaid agencies must cover most FDA-approved drugs and do not generally have the ability to demand price concessions in favor of coverage. Removing these two legal obstacles would have additional policy consequences not contemplated within the current policy discussion of these initiatives.

Transparency Laws

Several states are considering bills which would require pharmaceutical companies to report information on their research and development costs, marketing and advertising costs, and prices charged to a number of different purchasers. Vermont is the first state to have officially enacted such a law. Different states have crafted their bills in different ways, to apply to different classes of drugs at different times and to require the disclosure of different pieces of information.

These bills themselves do not directly constrain drug prices. However, they may serve to enable states to gather information that they can use to make such policy going forward. Alternatively, states like Vermont, which require justification for price increases, may use the laws to serve a "naming and shaming" function which has been demonstrated to hold down prices at least to some degree.

These are just a few of the many proposals that have been discussed with the potential to curb high drug prices. Others would tackle the issue indirectly, by attempting to speed FDA approval of competitor products or by limiting consumers' out-of-pocket expenditures.

In addition, the private sector is taking action on its own to encourage different types of value-based pricing for pharmaceuticals, with groups like the Institute for Clinical and Economic Review analyzing and providing critical public information on the value of many new products. But in the near term, these four proposals have the greatest possibility of becoming law and deserve our attention going forward.

> *"Political contributions, which are typically made by individuals and political action committees within a corporation, can curry favors from candidates in the future, but lobbying allows Big Pharma to take advantage of Washington's revolving door and directly influence legislation."*

Big Pharma Has Too Much Influence over Politicians

Mike Ludwig

In the following viewpoint, Mike Ludwig explains the relationship between the pharmaceutical industry and the US government, as big pharma companies are some of the largest contributors to political campaigns, according to data from the Center for Responsive Politics. Ludwig discusses how the pharmaceutical industry's lobbying expenditures steadily increased from 1998 to 2009, and how Pfizer and other large pharmaceutical companies rank near the top of the list in terms of political contributions during recent past elections. With two of the most powerful groups in the country doing their best to keep drug prices high, there is no definite end in sight. Mike Ludwig is a staff reporter at Truthout and a contributor to the Truthout anthology, Who Do You Serve, Who Do You Protect?

As you read, consider the following questions:

1. How much did Pfizer spend in federal campaign contributions during the 2014 elections?
2. For every $1 the industry spent on contributions during the last election cycle, how much was spent on lobbying in 2014?
3. What does PhRMA stand for?

W henever it's called out for charging too much for drugs or outright price gouging, the pharmaceutical industry's standard defense is to assure the public that its profits will be used to develop even better drugs in the future. Turing Pharmaceuticals CEO Martin Shkreli clung to that defense in late September when asked to explain his sudden decision to hike the price of a longstanding anti-parasitic drug by more than $700, prompting a collective eye roll among medical experts and an outraged public.

In reality, a good chunk of pharmaceutical "research and development" comes from the subsidized labs at universities and the National Institutes of Health, and now angry consumers and even some prominent politicians are demanding that the industry put its money where its mouth is.

Large pharmaceutical firms are some of the most profitable companies in the world, so what do they spend all their money on, besides advertising and hefty salaries for rich kid CEOs? Sure, some profits are reinvested to fund research and clinical trials, but hundreds of millions of dollars are also spent on political operations every year, and federal law requires that drug companies disclose this political spending to the public.

The government has long singled out the pharmaceutical industry for premium patent protections while leaving drug pricing up to the whims of the market, and consumers in the United States now pay some of the highest prices in the world for many life-saving drugs. Recent reports show that critical cancer medicines, for example, cost as much as 600 times more in the

United States than other countries. The industry has a clear interest in maintaining the political status quo.

Big Pharma Spends Millions on Political Contributions

Pharmaceutical and health product companies injected $51 million into the 2012 federal elections and nearly $32 million into the 2014 elections, according to the Center for Responsive Politics (CRP). The industry has already spent nearly $10 million on the 2016 elections and is expected to spend more, especially now that Democratic presidential candidates Hillary Clinton and Bernie Sanders have made drug prices a campaign issue with separate proposals to rein them in with new regulations.

Big Pharma tends to spend more on Republicans than Democrats, and the GOP benefited from 58 percent of the industry's federal contributions in 2012 and 2014 while Democrats received 42 percent, according to the CRP.

Perhaps unsurprisingly, it's a group of 18 House Democrats, not Republicans, who are demanding that the CEO of Valeant Pharmaceuticals, Michael Pearson, join Shkreli in front of the House Oversight Committee during the first week of October to answer questions about recent price hikes on two drugs produced by his company.

By the time this article was published, the committee's chair, Rep. Jason Chaffetz (R-Utah), had not responded to a letter from the Democrats requesting that Valeant be subpoenaed to provide Congress with documents related to the drastic price hikes. The pharmaceutical industry has contributed $198,000 to Chaffetz's campaign war chest during the course of his career, more than any other special interest group, although none of the contributions came directly from Valeant, which has focused its political resources on lobbying instead of direct contributions.

Industry giant Pfizer was the top spender among drug companies during the 2014 elections with $1.5 million in federal campaign contributions, followed closely by Amgen with $1.3 million and

McKesson Corp with $1.1 million. All three companies spent more on Republicans than Democrats that year.

One million dollars plus is a lot of money, but it pales in comparison to the annual salaries of the CEOs at some of these companies. Pfizer CEO Ian Read, for example, raked in more than $23 million in 2014, and Amgen CEO Robert Bradway made a cool $14 million, according to the industry publication FiercePharma.

It turns out that the pharmaceutical industry did not become one for the most powerful interests on Capitol Hill with campaign contributions alone. For every $1 the industry spent on contributions during the last election cycle, $7 were spent on lobbying in 2014.

More Money Spent on Lobbying

The pharmaceutical industry's lobbying expenditures steadily increased from 1998 to 2009, when spending hit a $273 million peak as Congress debated the Affordable Care Act, according to CRP. In 2014, drug companies and their lobbying groups spent $229 million influencing lawmakers, legislation and politicians.

The Pharmaceutical Research and Manufacturers of America (PhRMA), the industry's lead lobbying group, has spent nearly $150 million on lobbying since 2008, and ranks sixth among the nation's top lobbying spenders, outspending powerful interests like defense contractors and the oil and gas industry, according to records retrieved from the MapLight lobbying database. The group has spent more than $10 million on lobbying so far this year. In contrast, PhRMA made $491,000 in political contributions during the 2014 election cycle.

Pfizer ranks among the top 25 lobbying spenders in the nation, with $94 million spent since 2008 and $8.5 million spent in 2014 alone.

Political contributions, which are typically made by individuals and political action committees within a corporation, can curry favors from candidates in the future, but lobbying allows Big

Pharma to take advantage of Washington's revolving door and directly influence legislation.

Consistent themes quickly emerge when reviewing records filed by the industry's top lobbying groups, with patent and trademark policies, Medicare and Medicaid, and international trade all ranking as top issues for Big Pharma.

Strict patent and trademark laws in the United States allow pharmaceutical companies to maintain monopolies on drugs for up to 20 years before generics can enter the market and drive down prices. Other countries that manufacture drugs, such as India, have looser patent laws and sometimes allow select manufacturers to make generic versions of certain patented drugs in order to keep prices of live-saving treatments from going through the roof.

As Truthout has reported, the pharmaceutical lobby has aggressively lobbied Congress and the Obama administration's trade representatives to put pressure on India to tighten its patent laws, which have allowed the country to produce cheap drugs that developing countries rely on to combat diseases like HIV/AIDS and hepatitis C.

The pharmaceutical lobby has also repeatedly lobbied to prevent Medicare from negotiating drug prices with drug companies. The proposals floated by Clinton and Sanders would give Medicare the ability to negotiate drug prices and increase market competition by allowing US consumers to buy drugs from Canada, and Big Pharma is already going on the offensive.

In a recent statement to the press, PhRMA claimed Clinton's plan would "turn back the clock on medical innovation and halt progress against the diseases that patients fear most." The proposal, PhRMA claimed, would result in jobs cuts and fewer new treatments for patients.

Despite PhRMA's sensationalist rhetoric, the industry has reportedly shrugged Clinton's plan off as a political long shot that would have little chance of passing Congress even if the Democrat is successful in taking the White House. Experts recently told The

Associated Press that Congress has repeatedly rejected Clinton's ideas over the past two decades.

In the meantime, high drug prices will continue to help drug companies gather the financial resources necessary to ensure that lawmakers do not change their minds.

> "Unlike in most other Western nations, drugmakers in the U.S. face no limits on the prices they can charge — and those prices have steadily increased over time."

Transparency Bills Are the Key to Lowering Drug Prices

Michael Ollove

In the following viewpoint, Michael Ollove reports on US lawmakers who are taking a stand against pharmaceutical price gouging. The author notes that lawmakers in various US states have started legislation that would require drug makers to disclose how much money they spent on research and development, manufacturing, and marketing of their drugs, in the hopes of making big pharmaceutical companies justify their pricing. The goal of this legislation—which are being called "transparency bills"—is to help attain lower drug prices in addition to educating consumers on the reasons for high drug costs, among other things. But will such bills ultimately help consumers? That remains to be seen. Ollove is an award-winning writer and reporter who covers health care for Stateline, an initiative of the Pew Charitable Trusts.

"High Drug Prices Prompt Demands for Transparency," by Michael Ollove, The Pew Charitable Trusts, March 7, 2016. Reprinted by permission.

As you read, consider the following questions:

1. The prices of medications rose what percent between 2006 and 2013?
2. Prescription drugs account for how much of health care spending in the US?
3. Tufts University's Center for the Study of Drug Development, which is largely funded by pharmaceutical and biotechnology firms, says it costs on average how many billions out-of-pocket to bring a new drug to market?

Outraged by exorbitant prices for certain prescription drugs, lawmakers in at least 11 states have introduced legislation that would require pharmaceutical companies to justify their prices by disclosing how much they spend on research, manufacturing and marketing.

The bills are similar to a provision in President Barack Obama's proposed 2017 budget.

The sponsors of the measures say they have a variety of goals: to educate policymakers and consumers about the reason for high prescription drug prices; to shame pharmaceutical companies into moderating their prices; and, in some states, including Massachusetts, to actually place a ceiling on prices that are determined to be unjustified.

"They are price-gouging," said Massachusetts state Sen. Mark Montigny, the assistant majority leader and the author of a transparency measure in that state. The Democrat said he hopes the disclosures will embarrass drugmakers into setting their prices at levels that would make the drugs affordable to those who need them. "We not only have a right but a responsibility to push back on this special interest and say, 'Hey, you've got to justify your price.' "

Unlike in most other Western nations, drugmakers in the U.S. face no limits on the prices they can charge—and those prices have steadily increased over time. The prices of medications rose 9.4 percent between 2006 and 2013, compared to a general inflation rate of 1.5 percent, according to the AARP. Spending on prescription drugs rose by 12.2 percent in 2014, while overall health care spending grew by 5.3 percent, according to the federal government.

And all health care payers—from individuals and private insurers to the federal government and the state— are grappling with how to meet those rising costs.

In addition to Massachusetts, transparency measures have been filed or carried over from last year in Colorado, Michigan, North Carolina, Oregon, Pennsylvania, Tennessee, Virginia and Washington. A proposal in New York has the strong support of Democratic Gov. Andrew Cuomo, while one in California was defeated in early January. Unusually in these days of hyper-partisanship, some of the bills have been filed by Republicans and some by Democrats.

"Trust Us"

A handful of transparency bills were filed last year, but none of them passed. But advocates like Montigny say continued revelations about high prices have only strengthened support for such legislation.

A generation of new drugs to cure hepatitis C, with a price tag as high as $95,000 for a course of treatment, as well as medications for some unusual forms of cancer that cost more than $100,000 a year, have drawn public scrutiny—and outrage.

Then there is the case of Martin Shkreli, a young pharmaceutical entrepreneur who raised the price of a medicine that eliminates a particular parasite that threatens the lives of some AIDS patients from $13.50 to $750 per tablet.

Presidential candidates from both parties have also lambasted pharmaceutical companies for exorbitant drug prices.

For now, those prices are a mystery that the industry has no interest in solving, said Leigh Purvis, director of health services research at AARP's Public Policy Institute. "It's basically a 'trust us' situation."

The bills on transparency, Purvis said, demonstrate that the "trust us" approach is no longer satisfying consumers, policymakers, insurers, physician organizations and advocates for better health care access.

The pharmaceutical industry has so far been successful at fending off efforts to control how it sets prices, while keeping a tight lid on any information that would reveal how it arrives at those prices. It has even managed to block Medicare, the second biggest health plan behind Medicaid, from the ability to negotiate better prices for its 50 million beneficiaries.

The industry insists that it is being unfairly targeted by the transparency measures, pointing out that prescription drugs account for only 10 percent of health care spending in the United States, $300 billion out of $3 trillion per year.

Industry representatives also say the information being sought is proprietary and has little to do with the actual price drug companies charge. Pricing, said Priscilla VanderVeer, a spokeswoman for the Pharmaceutical Research and Manufacturers of America, the industry's main lobbying group, is more related to the marketplace, to competition, and to how beneficial the drugs are.

Drugmakers say only a small fraction of drugs entering clinical trials eventually gain approval from the U.S. Food and Drug Administration—7 percent, according to one study. Those that make it to market pay for research and development of the next generation of breakthrough drugs, which will also involve trial and error, VanderVeer said. That's the way innovative therapies happen, she said.

Tufts University's Center for the Study of Drug Development, which is largely funded by pharmaceutical and biotechnology firms, says it costs on average $1.4 billion out-of-pocket to bring a new drug to market.

The Effect of Price Controls on Pharmaceutical Research

For the pharmaceutical industry, one economic problem is that only 3 out of every 10 of their products generate after-tax returns (measured in present value terms) in excess of average, after-tax R and D costs. The scientific process is heavily regulated, and involves significant technical risk. Only one in several thousand compounds investigated ever makes it through the full development process to gain approval of the Food and Drug Administration. The vast majority of R and D projects fail for reasons related to safety, efficacy, or commercial viability, the authors note. For compounds that do gain FDA approval and are taken to market, the entire process from discovery to launch takes on average about 15 years.

Further, it's estimated that the pre-tax cost of a new drug runs around $802 million. The after-tax cost of an average drug is about $480 million, assuming the company has sufficient revenues to take advantage of the tax benefits or can somehow sell the tax benefits to another firm. The average net revenues for a new drug amount to about $525 million in present value. Thus at the time of a product launch, the drug company can foresee a potential average profit or economic value for their pharmaceutical R and D of about $45 million.

With this economic scene as background, a company must make a financial decision about whether to take an R and D project into clinical development. This step is called the Phase 1 Go/No-Go decision. Only one out of five projects that are given the "Go" signal into clinical development actually reach the market as a product. Factoring in this uncertainty, the authors write, is essential to understanding the behavior of the industry. This uncertainty factor may explain what critics say is a tendency of the pharmaceutical industry to focus on only minor innovations (me-too products) because of their greater probability of success, at the expense of conducting more revolutionary research that carries a higher risk of failure but also may yield greater health improvements.

"The Effect of Price Controls on Pharmaceutical Research," by David R. Francis, National Bureau of Economic Research, May 23, 2017.

Earlier Measures

In legislative fights across the country, two well-heeled and influential industries are pitted against each other. The pharmaceutical industry has contributed $9.6 million to the campaigns of state lawmakers since 2014, while the insurance industry has spent $21 million, according to the National Institute on Money in State Politics, a nonprofit that tracks campaign donations.

VanderVeer, of the pharmaceutical manufacturers group, says the whole pricing issue has been generated by insurance companies. She characterizes the transparency bills as "a somewhat cynical attempt to rile up pharma by insurance."

Clare Krusing, a spokeswoman for America's Health Insurance Plans, which represents commercial insurers, said the proposed legislation represents common-sense public policy: "Health plans have to make rates public and they are scrutinized by consumers and regulators so it's clear where every dollar of premium is going. We don't have that with drug pricing."

Colorado state Rep. Joann Ginal, a Democrat, said her transparency bill has attracted wide support: from health plans, consumer organizations, labor and senior citizen organizations and county governments.

Drugmakers have also enlisted some supporters. In Colorado, their allies include manufacturing groups and social service organizations that advocate on behalf of those with some diseases, such as the Partnership to Fight Chronic Disease and the Liver Health Connection. Eileen Doherty, executive director of the Colorado Gerontological Society, a nonprofit serving the elderly, said that although high drug prices are a major burden for the people she serves, "I don't see any reason why the bill as written would make any difference."

But Ginal says drug prices have simply reached a tipping point and it's time that policymakers understand why. "I know lives have been saved" by prescription medications, she said. "But I can't stand by as these needed medications become out of range for people who need them."

The transparency bills are only the latest front in states' attempts to deal with high medication prices. Before this year's legislative session, at least seven states had capped the amount insurance companies could require patients to pay out-of-pocket for biologics, a class of extremely complex and usually expensive medicines made from organic materials that are most commonly prescribed for certain cancers and auto-immune and nervous system disorders.

Price Ceilings?

The bills around the country are not all the same, and they are likely to change as they move through the legislative process. Most contain some kind of price trigger that would require drugmakers to disclose information about cost. For example, Ginal's bill would only affect drugs that are priced above $50,000 for a course of treatment or annual supply. Although lawmakers, regulators and consumers would have access to the information, the drug would not be subject to any further government action, such as price setting, under her bill.

"What we need to do is look at why the prices are as high as they are, and I believe without that consumers and policymakers are unable to enter into a discussion about pricing," Ginal said.

But under Montigny's bill in Massachusetts, if regulators found that the price set by a manufacturer was unjustified, they could set a maximum allowable price for that drug in the state. (The measures to be used to assess the price have not yet been developed.)

Montigny doesn't mince words when speaking about the pharmaceutical industry. Other parts of the health care system, such as hospitals, must explain how they set their prices, and there's no reason drugmakers should stand apart, he said. "Why should everyone else be in the spotlight in health care but them?"

Some experts in drug pricing who are sympathetic to the goals of the transparency bills are dubious that they will accomplish what their sponsors hope.

"There is a problem in trying to attack the problem this way," said Kenneth Kaitin, director of the Tufts Center for the Study of Drug Development.

It would be difficult for drugmakers to supply cost information because many of their products are the result of mergers, acquisitions and partnerships, Kaitin said. As for the information that is available, he said even an accountant would find it hard to understand, let alone a lawmaker or a regulator. The proposed bills would seek information about government subsidies and the costs of clinical trials, patent acquisition, advertising, manufacturing and distribution.

Beyond that, Kaitin agrees with industry officials that the cost associated with research and development, manufacturing and marketing are not really relevant to the price drugmakers charge.

"My fear is a lot of energy and emotion is tied up in these proposals to get at drug pricing and in the end it's just not going to make a difference," Kaitin said.

But Kaitin said the bills may accomplish something else.

By talking about pricing and transparency, Kaitin said, lawmakers may pressure the industry into talking with policymakers, health plans and others with a stake in health care about "how to make sure tomorrow's breakthrough drugs are affordable and accessible to the patients who need them."

> *"There's no mystery why prescription drug prices are higher in the U.S.: virtually every country regulates prices and the U.S. doesn't. In fact, Congress has explicitly prohibited Medicare from negotiating drug prices with pharmaceutical companies."*

It's Time to Rein in Exorbitant Pharmaceutical Prices

Rafi Mohammed

In the following viewpoint, Rafi Mohammed argues that pharmaceutical companies are not to blame for high drug costs, but rather the Congress holds ultimate responsibility, as it has allowed this practice to continue. Mohammed writes that drug companies are operating within the rules and restraints that have been set by the US government. Mohammed's solution to high drug prices is regulation. Regulators could pass a law that would state that insurance companies and government agencies wouldn't pay more than a set percentage above or below what other developed countries pay for drugs. Mohammed is a pricing strategy consultant and author of The 1% Windfall: How Successful Companies Use Price to Profit and Grow.

"It's Time to Rein in Exorbitant Pharmaceutical Prices," by Rafi Mohammed, Harvard Business School Publishing, September 22, 2015. Reprinted by permission.

As you read, consider the following questions:

1. Prices for drugs in advanced countries are often what percentage cheaper than what Americans pay for drugs?
2. Prices for commonly used brand name prescription drugs in the US rose by how many times the general inflation rate in 2013?
3. Nine out the top ten pharma companies spend more on what than research and development?

A s the ire over high prescription drug prices in the United States escalates, it's easy to blame pharmaceutical companies. But pharmaceutical companies aren't to blame. They've executed well on the rules set by the U.S. government as well as the "make the most money" dictum set by their stockholders. Over the last five years, returns for the S&P Pharmaceuticals Select Industry Index have been virtually double that of the S&P 500 (roughly 24% vs. 12% annually).

But blaming them for their high prices is short-sighted finger pointing. Americans need to take some responsibility for deciding how drug prices are set, and they need to ask the larger question for the future: how should future pharmaceutical advancements be funded?

American drug prices are among the highest in the world. Prices in advanced countries are often 50% cheaper than what Americans pay for drugs. The AARP estimates prices for commonly used brand name prescription drugs in the U.S. rose by 8 times the general inflation rate in 2013. The annual expense for a recently developed cancer drug cocktail is $295,000. (No wonder health insurance expenses are one of the biggest costs facing many employers.)

There's no mystery why prescription drug prices are higher in the U.S.: virtually every country regulates prices and the U.S. doesn't. In fact, Congress has explicitly prohibited Medicare from negotiating drug prices with pharmaceutical companies. (Close to

40 million people in the U.S. have this prescription drug benefit). Prices in Norway, the fourth wealthiest country in the world (U.S. is number 6), for instance, are amongst the lowest in Western Europe. The bottom line: most countries play hardball on drug prices, while the U.S. pays retail. As a result, consumers in the U.S. are stuck footing most of the bill for developing new drugs, even as consumers throughout the developed world reap the benefits.

I believe in the free market and rarely advocate any type of price regulation. There are compelling reasons, however, to consider doing so for pharmaceuticals. The biggest expense of a new drug is R&D; once developed, the cost of producing pills is relatively trivial. Most important, everyone in the world can – and should – benefit from pharmaceutical advancements, especially since the variable costs are so low. In other words, the R&D behind new drugs is a *common good.* Typical solutions to the dilemma of high drug prices include single payer (e.g., U.S. government negotiates "take it or leave it" prices for its territory) and price regulation (e.g., the government simply specifies prices). These tactics will lower prices but don't address the issue of paying for new pharmaceutical developments. How can we make sure that the cost of developing new drugs is equitably split among the various beneficiaries around the world? That high-price-paying Americans are not essentially subsidizing R&D for pharma multinationals?

A tethered price regulation is the answer. Regulators could pass a law that says neither American insurers nor government agencies would pay more than a set percentage above (or below) what other developed countries pay for drugs. In other words, our prices are tethered to theirs. This accomplishes two goals. First, drug prices will be lowered for Americans. Second and just as importantly, pharma companies and other countries will be on notice that sick Americans are no longer going to shoulder a disproportionate share of drug development costs. Tethered regulation should apply only to new drugs, not existing drugs, which were developed with the understanding that U.S. prices

Is Canada the Answer?

Why are drug prices so much higher in the U.S.? The answer is straightforward: most countries regulate prices or have a single-payer health care system, in which the government pays for citizens' health care costs. In a single-payer system, the government buys all a country's pharmaceuticals, and it has leverage in "take it or leave it" negotiations with pharma companies.

In contrast, the U.S. doesn't regulate drug prices, nor does it have a single-payer system. As a result, each U.S. health-related entity (primarily insurance companies) has to individually negotiate with pharmaceutical companies, which leads to higher prices for two reasons. First, no U.S. health insurance player is big enough to play pricing hardball with drug manufacturers. Just as important, to keep their plans competitive, insurance companies are under pressure to make deals to provide the best medicines to their policy holders. So in contrast to prices being dictated by foreign countries, drug companies have the upper hand in U.S. negotiations. What results is the intended outcome of differential pricing: different countries pay different prices for the same drug, with U.S. citizens paying a hefty premium.

To understand why importing drugs from Canada won't result in lower prices, let's return to the cinema. Suppose you own a movie theater and notice groups of students are reselling their discounted tickets in the lobby to customers who normally pay full price. What would you do? Probably discontinue the discounts or impose restrictions to limit the arbitrage. This is exactly how pharmaceutical executives will react if Americans start importing large quantities of drugs from Canada. New restrictions will be attached to discounted Canadian deals. For example, exports will be banned, or quantities sold at a discount will be limited (enough to cover citizens), with amounts over the limit being charged full price. Poof, there goes the grand plan to lower American drug prices.

Policy makers need to realize that importing drugs from Canada will result in the equivalent of a whack-a-mole pricing game. Pharmaceutical companies will quickly and easily amend strategies to close the discount loophole. After all, drug companies are for-profit companies with a mandate from investors to earn the highest profits.

"Cheap Drugs from Canada Won't Reduce U.S. Drug Prices," by Rafi Mohammed, Harvard Business School Publishing, February 12, 2016.

will be as high as the market can bear. We made a bad deal, but we should keep our word.

A common reaction to any whiff of price regulation is concern that pharma R&D will be reduced. This is a fair concern, but it's not a given that R&D will decrease. Pharma companies may opt to cut sales and marketing costs (which 9 out the top 10 pharma companies spend more on than R&D), executive compensation, or dividends instead, keeping R&D budgets healthy. That said, it is very possible R&D may decrease as a result of regulation. In utopia, it'd be wonderful for pharma companies to have unlimited R&D budgets. But back here in reality, tradeoffs are made. Even today, R&D budgets are not infinite. And if budgets are cut by 20%, instead of funding 100 initiatives, it may be that only the top 80 with the highest potential will be greenlit.

The word "regulation" and threats of lower pharma R&D can be polarizing. There's room for a more balanced discussion: regulation *may be* appropriate for select products, the possibility of lower R&D *may be* acceptable in return for lower costs and expanded access to important drugs. Now is the time to have this crucial discussion. And if the U.S. decides to keep the status quo – that's fine. But in that case, Americans should recognize that we have *chosen* to keep prices high and subsidize drug development for the rest of the world, rather than pointing the finger at pharmaceutical executives.

> *"The bottom line is that the government can and does get better deals on drugs than private purchasers. The effects of these policies on quality and innovation need to be better understood—but were the government to expand them, it would be more of an evolution than a revolution."*

The Government Doesn't Deserve the Blame for High Drug Prices

David Blumenthal, MD, and David Squires

In the following viewpoint, David Blumenthal and David Squires defend the US government by stating that the federal government has deployed tools to reduce prices of drugs purchased by certain public programs, including Medicaid, the 340B Program, the Veterans Health Administration (VA), and the Department of Defense (DOD). The authors conclude their article by reminding the reader that at the end of the day, the government achieves better deals on drugs than private purchasers, and that should these policies be expanded, it could only evolve where America goes with lowering drug prices. Blumenthal is president of the Commonwealth Fund, a national philanthropy engaged in independent research on health and social policy issues. Squires is his former senior researcher.

"Drug Price Control: How Some Government Programs Do It," by David Blumenthal, M.D. and David Squires, The Commonwealth Fund, May 10, 2016. Reprinted by permission.

As you read, consider the following questions:

1. What is the purpose of the 340B Program?
2. What are the two broad categories listed by the writers that the federal government employs to help reduce drug prices purchased by public programs?
3. Medicare Part B reimburses doctors and hospitals what percent of the average sales prices for a given drug?

Drug pricing is having its moment. Thousand-dollar pills to treat Hepatitis C, eye-popping price hikes for common generics, and surging overall spending on pharmaceuticals have rung alarm bells from coast to coast. All the while, drugs continue to be up to twice as expensive in the U.S. as in other wealthy countries. Proposed treatments for the drug pricing epidemic are varied, but some call for government to do more.

While others resist the idea of government involvement, the federal government, in fact, already employs a number of effective tools for reducing the prices of drug purchased by certain public programs. These fall into two broad categories:

1. Price controls, usually in the form of required discounts off of the average price paid by other purchasers.
2. Negotiated pricing, in which the government wields its market power to bargain for favorable rates from pharmaceutical suppliers.

These strategies do not exhaust the available approaches, nor are they necessarily the most desirable. But as the current drug pricing discussion evolves, it's worth reviewing the nature and track record of the government's existing drug price reduction efforts.

The Programs

Medicaid
While the details differ by state, Medicaid's drug pricing strategies are mostly based on discounts that drug manufacturers are required to give on retail drugs. In effect, these rebates lower the prices paid by Medicaid to whichever is lower: 23.1 percent less than the average price paid for the drug by other buyers, or the lowest price at which the drug is sold to other buyers. Medicaid gets an additional rebate if a drug's price rises faster than inflation. In addition to these mandatory rebates, state Medicaid programs can negotiate further discounts.

The Veterans Health Administration (VA) and the Department of Defense (DOD)
The VA and DOD require that drug manufacturers offer them a discounted price—equal to 24 percent off of a drug's average price or the lowest price paid by other (nonfederal) buyers— as well as further discounts if a drug's price outstrips inflation. The two programs also directly negotiate lower prices with drug manufacturers. They may engage in these negotiations separately, or combine their substantial market share and negotiate together.

Both programs also use formularies to manage which drugs they cover. These formularies strengthen their negotiating stance. By threatening to offer only limited coverage for a drug, or to leave it off of the formulary entirely, the VA and DOD are able to extract steeper discounts from manufacturers. (Though as a practical matter, and as a matter of law, both programs cover drugs that are medically necessary.)

340B Program
Little-known outside policy circles, the 340B Program (named after section 340B of the Public Health Service Act, which authorizes it) requires drug manufacturers to offer discounts on outpatient drugs to certain hospitals, community health centers, and other facilities that treat large numbers of low-income patients. These

discounts are available for drugs dispensed by a 340B provider, or for drugs dispensed by an outside pharmacy that has contracted with a 340B provider. For the most part, these discounts are similar to the rebates in the Medicaid program.

The 340B Program also works with a private company called a "prime vendor" to negotiate even steeper markdowns. Because the combined market share of 340B providers is quite large—roughly 45 percent of all hospitals participate—the prime vendor can sometimes negotiate better deals with drug manufacturers than the mandated discounts.

Medicare Part B?

On the topic of drug pricing and public programs, we'd be remiss not to mention the Centers for Medicare and Medicaid Services' recently proposed pricing change for drugs administered under Medicare Part B. Currently, Part B reimburses doctors and hospitals 106 percent of the average sales prices for a given drug—the extra 6 percent serves as a fee to account for providers' nonmedication costs, or overhead. The concern is that the 6 percent fee is larger for an expensive drug than a cheaper drug, providing a financial incentive for doctors to prescribe pricier medication. Under the proposed model, the fee would instead be 2.5 percent of a drug's price plus a flat rate of $16.80.

So, contrary to how it has at times been described, the proposed change is not an attempt to reduce drug prices paid by the Part B program directly. Rather, it aims to remove an unintended financial incentive under the current system for health professionals to provide highly expensive pharmaceuticals. Because the proposed reform has prompted considerable opposition from providers and elected officials, its fate remains uncertain. A second phase of the proposed Part B payment model, which aims to encourage value-based prescribing, may include some elements that reduce drug prices for the program. However, the details for this phase have yet to be laid out.

The Effects?

The strategies described above clearly result in cheaper drugs for the VA, DOD, Medicaid, and 340B providers. The Congressional Budget Office has estimated that the VA and DOD pay drug prices that are roughly half as much as those paid by retail pharmacies, and that Medicaid pays about one-third less than Medicare Part D (which pays whatever prices its plans negotiate in private markets). The agency that runs the 340B program estimates that it reduces drug prices for participating providers by one-third.

The bottom line is that the government can and does get better deals on drugs than private purchasers. The effects of these policies on quality and innovation need to be better understood—but were the government to expand them, it would be more of an evolution than a revolution.

> *"One of the ways branded drug manufacturers prevent competition is simple: cash. In so-called 'pay for delay' agreements, a brand drug company simply pays a generic company not to launch a version of a drug. The Federal Trade Commission estimates these pacts cost U.S. consumers and taxpayers $3.5 billion in higher drug costs each year."*

Pharma Companies Game the System to Keep Drugs Expensive

Erin Fox

In the following viewpoint, Erin Fox gives readers a first-hand look at how pharmaceutical companies game the system. Since she helps manage drug budgets and medication use policies for the University of Utah hospital system, she receives consistent sticker shock as drug costs continue to skyrocket. The author ultimately comes to the conclusion that this type of unpredictable inflation isn't sustainable and isn't how America is supposed to work. Generics are one way for consumers to save money, but branded drug manufacturers do everything in their power to make sure that the branded drugs are what consumers are receiving, which means high drug costs. Fox, Pharm.D., BCPS, FASHP, is director of drug information at University of Utah Health in Salt Lake City.

"How Pharma Companies Game the System to Keep Drugs Expensive," by Erin Fox, Harvard Business School Publishing, April 6, 2017. Reprinted by permission.

As you read, consider the following questions:

1. What did the 1984 Drug Price Competition and Patent Term Restoration Act do?
2. By law, the first generic company to market a drug gets an exclusivity period of how many days?
3. How many generic drug products were recalled in 2015?

I help the University of Utah hospital system manage its drug budgets and medication use policies, and in 2015 I got sticker shock. Our annual inpatient pharmacy cost for a single drug skyrocketed from $300,000 to $1.9 million. That's because the drug maker Valeant suddenly increased the price of isoproterenol from $440 to roughly $2,700 a dose.

Isoproterenol is a heart drug. It helps with heart attacks and shock and works to keep up a patient's blood pressure. With the sudden price increase, we were forced to remove isoproterenol from our 100 emergency crash carts. Instead, we stocked our pharmacy backup boxes, located on each floor of our hospitals, to have the vital drug on hand if needed. We had to minimize costs without impacting patient care.

This type of arbitrary and unpredictable inflation is not sustainable. And it's not the way things are supposed to work in the United States. Isoproterenol is a drug that is no longer protected by a patent. Theoretically, any drug company should be able to make a generic version and sell it at a competitive cost. We should have had other options to buy a competitors' copy for $440 or less. But that's not happening like it should. The promise of generic medications is getting further from reality each day. As the U.S. Senate considers President Donald Trump's choice to head the Food and Drug Administration, now is the time to refocus efforts on generic drugs.

How Generics Are Supposed to Work

The 1984 Drug Price Competition and Patent Term Restoration Act gave pharmaceutical companies exclusive protections for innovating a new drug. If they brought a new therapy to life, they enjoyed patent protection to effectively monopolize the market. That was the payoff for shouldering the high risk and high costs of developing new drugs.

But once the patent and the exclusive hold on the market expires, the legislation encouraged competition to benefit consumers. Any drug company would be able to manufacture non-brand name versions of the very same drug, so-called "generics." And for a while, the system worked well.

Not anymore. The system intended to reward drug companies for their innovations, but eventually protect consumers, is systematically being broken. Drug companies are thwarting competition through a number of tactics, and the result is high prices, little to no competition, and drug quality problems.

The Ways Companies Stop Generics

One of the ways branded drug manufacturers prevent competition is simple: cash. In so-called "pay for delay" agreements, a brand drug company simply pays a generic company not to launch a version of a drug. The Federal Trade Commission estimates these pacts cost U.S. consumers and taxpayers $3.5 billion in higher drug costs each year.

"Citizen petitions" offer drug companies another way to delay generics from being approved. These ask the Food and Drug Administration to delay action on a pending generic drug application. By law, the FDA is required to prioritize these petitions. However, the citizens filing concerns are not individuals, they're corporations. The FDA recently said branded drug manufacturers submitted 92% of all citizen petitions. Many of these petitions are filed near the date of patent expiration, effectively limiting potential competition for another 150 days.

"Authorized generics" are another tactic to limit competition. These aren't really generic products at all; they are the same product sold under a generic name by the company that sells the branded drug. Why? By law, the first generic company to market a drug gets an exclusivity period of 180 days. During this time, no other companies can market a generic product. But the company with the expiring patent is not barred from launching an "authorized generic." By selling a drug they're already making under a different name, pharmaceutical firms are effectively extending their monopoly for another six months.

Another way pharmaceutical firms are thwarting generics is by restricting access to samples for testing. Generic drug makers need to be able to purchase a sample of a brand-name product to conduct bioequivalence testing. That's because they have to prove they can make a bioequivalent product following the current good manufacturing practices (CGMP) standard. These manufacturers don't need to conduct clinical trials like the original drug company did.

But the original drug developer often declines to sell drug samples to generics manufacturers by citing "FDA requirements," by which they mean the agency's Risk Evaluation and Mitigation Strategies program. The idea behind this program is a good one: give access to patients who will benefit from these personalized medicines, and bar access for patients who won't benefit and could be seriously harmed. However, brand drug makers are citing these requirements for the sole purpose of keeping generics from coming to market.

Problems with Generic Drug Makers

Although makers of a branded drug are using a variety of tactics to create barriers to healthy competition, generic drug companies are often not helping their own case. In 2015, there were 267 recalls of generic drug products—more than one every other day. These recalls are for quality issues such as products not dissolving properly, becoming contaminated, or even being outright counterfeits.

A few high-profile recalls have shaken the belief that generic drugs are truly the same. In 2014, the FDA withdrew approval of Budeprion XL 300 — Teva's generic version of GlaxoSmithKline's Wellbutrin XL. Testing showed the drug did not properly release its key ingredient, substantiating consumers' claims that the generic was not equivalent. In addition, concerns about contaminated generic Lipitor caused the FDA to launch a $20 million initiative to test generic products to ensure they are truly therapeutically equivalent.

In some cases, patent law also collides with the FDA's manufacturing rules. For example, the Novartis patent for Diovan expired in 2012. Ranbaxy received exclusivity for 180 days for the first generic product. However, due to poor quality manufacturing, Ranbaxy couldn't obtain final FDA approval for its generic version. The FDA banned shipments of Ranbaxy products to the United States. Ranbaxy ended up paying a $500 million fine, the largest penalty paid by a generic firm for violations.

Due to these protracted problems with the company that had won exclusivity, a generic product did not become available until 2014. The two-year delay cost Medicare and Medicaid at least $900 million. Ranbaxy's poor-quality manufacturing also delayed other key generic products like Valcyte and Nexium. Ironically, it was Mylan—involved in its own drug pricing scandal over its EpiPen allergy-reaction injector—that filed the first lawsuit to have the FDA strip Ranbaxy of its exclusivity. Mylan made multiple attempts to produce generic products but was overruled in the courts.

Ways to Fix the System

Pharmaceutical firms are currently using a set of tactics to make their temporary monopolies semi-permanent. Eliminating these tactics will not be easy. Still, doing so will fulfill the deal that policy makers offered to drug makers and consumers: a *temporary* monopoly on sales to help pay for drug development.

First, restrictive distribution programs need to be stopped. Generic companies must also be allowed to purchase samples of these medications to conduct bioequivalence studies. (One measure to close these loopholes already has bipartisan support.) Next, pay-for-delay agreements should be eliminated as well as a corporation's ability to issue citizen petitions with the intent of delaying generic competition.

Encouraging and enforcing high-quality standards for medications must also be an industry imperative. To create transparency around drug quality, the FDA has proposed a system of letter grades for manufacturers. In an economic study, one official notes that lack of transparency "may have produced a market situation in which quality problems have become sufficiently common and severe to result in drug shortages."

Another way to achieve greater transparency in medication quality is to change the product labeling laws. Labels should disclose the medication's manufacturer. Currently, hospitals and pharmacies don't always know which company actually made the product. This makes it difficult to base purchase decisions on quality.

Generic medications can provide great benefits for patients and health systems when there is adequate competition and quality. But their promise is unfulfilled, and it's costing consumers. By eliminating restrictive distribution schemes, pay-for-delay, and citizen petitions as well as providing more transparency around quality, hospitals, clinicians, lawmakers, and the new leaders at the FDA have a clear opportunity. They can start to reverse rising health care costs and ensure quality medications are accessible to the American people.

Periodical and Internet Sources Bibliography

The following articles have been selected to supplement the diverse views presented in this chapter.

Anna Edney, "Trump calls drug pricing 'astronomical' and promises changes," The Chicago Tribune, January 31, 2017. http://www.chicagotribune.com/business/ct-trump-drugmakers-price-controls-20170131-story.html.

Yevgeniy Feyman, "Vermont's Wrongheaded Drug Price 'Transparency' Bill Misses The Mark," Forbes, June 10, 2016. https://www.forbes.com/sites/theapothecary/2016/06/10/vermonts-wrongheaded-drug-price-transparency-bill-misses-the-mark/#6573c7de7bf7.

Carolyn Johnson, "Trump calls for lower drug prices, fewer regulations in meeting with pharmaceutical executives," The Washington Post, January 31, 2017. https://www.washingtonpost.com/news/wonk/wp/2017/01/31/trump-calls-for-lower-drug-prices-fewer-regulations-in-meeting-with-pharmaceutical-executives/?utm_term=.2c907cfd0079.

Carolyn Johnson, "Trump on drug prices: Pharma companies are 'getting away with murder,'" The Washington Post, January 11, 2017. https://www.washingtonpost.com/news/wonk/wp/2017/01/11/trump-on-drug-prices-pharma-companies-are-getting-away-with-murder/?utm_term=.71f594c329dc.

Rachel King and Doug Doerfler, "Md. drug pricing transparency bill misunderstands U.S. medicine market," The Baltimore Sun, February 22, 2017. http://www.baltimoresun.com/news/opinion/oped/bs-ed-drug-pricing-con-20170222-story.html.

Alison Noon, "Nevada Senate Passes Insulin-Price Bill Tough on Drugmakers," U.S. News, May 19, 2017. https://www.usnews.com/news/best-states/nevada/articles/2017-05-19/nevada-senate-passes-insulin-price-bill-tough-on-drugmakers.

Lydia Ramsey, "Nevada just passed one of the strictest drug pricing transparency laws in the country," Business Insider, June 15, 2017. http://www.businessinsider.com/nevada-passes-insulin-drug-pricing-transparency-bill-2017-6.

Alexander Schuhmacher, Oliver Gassmann, and Markus Hinder, "Changing R&D models in research-based pharmaceutical companies," NCBI, Apr. 27, 2016. https://www.ncbi.nlm.nih.gov/pmc/articles/PMC4847363.

Katie Thomas, "A Look at Major Drug-Pricing Proposals," The New York Times, May 29, 2017. https://www.nytimes.com/2017/05/29/health/a-look-at-major-drug-pricing-proposals.html.

Katie Thomas, "The Fight Trump Faces Over Drug Prices," The New York Times, January 23, 2017. https://www.nytimes.com/2017/01/23/health/the-fight-trump-faces-over-drug-prices.html.

Sarah Jane Tribble and Sydney Lupkin, "GOP Senators Ask GAO To Investigate High Prices For Orphan Drugs," NPR, March 7, 2017. http://www.npr.org/sections/health-shots/2017/03/07/518980280/gop-senators-ask-gao-to-investigate-high-prices-for-orphan-drugs.

Jessica Wapner, "Trump's Plan for Lowering Big Pharma Drug Prices Comes at a High Cost," Newsweek, February 3, 2017. http://www.newsweek.com/trump-drug-prices-big-pharma-552295.

Robert Weisman, "Four bills ask Legislature to target high drug prices," The Boston Globe, January 24, 2017. https://www.bostonglobe.com/business/2017/01/24/four-bills-beacon-hill-target-drug-pricing/ot0P13whyDRuzCY6I5hsEN/story.html.

For Further Discussion

Chapter 1

1. Are prescription drugs priced fairly in the United States? Why or why not?
2. What role does higher education play in the pharmaceutical industry? Explain the other impacts of drug prices.
3. Why does it take so long to bring generic drugs to market?

Chapter 2

1. How are medically necessary drugs contributing to drug pricing increases?
2. How can employers of larger corporations help to reduce the costs of prescription drugs for their employees?
3. How does the US government impact and contribute to the high costs of drugs? What can it do to lower prices for Americans?

Chapter 3

1. Why do Americans spend more on prescription drugs than other countries?
2. How has the demand for prescription drugs contributed to higher costs?
3. Should pharmaceutical companies be allowed to profit at consumers' expense? Does the work these companies do balance out the prices they charge?

Chapter 4

1. What are transparency bills and how would they benefit consumers?
2. How does US government policy promote high drug costs?
3. What should the government do to protect its citizens from astronomically-priced medication?

Organizations to Contact

The editors have compiled the following list of organizations concerned with the issues debated in this book. The descriptions are derived from materials provided by the organizations. All have publications or information available for interested readers. The list was compiled on the date of publication of the present volume; the information provided here may change. Be aware that many organizations take several weeks or longer to respond to inquiries, so allow as much time as possible.

American Civil Liberties Union
125 Broad Street, 18th Floor
New York, NY 10004
(212) 549-2500
website: http://www.aclu.org

The American Civil Liberties Union is an organization made up of more than 1.6 million members. The ACLU fights government abuse in various areas, including the health care landscape in America. The ACLU has been in existence for nearly 100 years and continues to fight for freedom in many areas for US citizens.

American Public Health Association
800 I Street, NW
Washington, DC 20001
(202) 777-2742
email: mediarelations@apha.org
website: http://www.apha.org

The American Public Health Association is a non-profit organization that speaks out for public health issues on behalf of Americans across the country. It claims to be the only organization to influence federal policy, also toting 145 years of perspective on the subject. The APHA publishes the American Journal of Public Health and The Nation's Health newspaper.

Center for American Progress
1333 H Street NW, 10th Floor
Washington, D.C., 20005
(202) 682-1611
website: http://www.americanprogress.org/

The Center for American Progress is an independent nonpartisan policy institute that has a goal to make America a better place across various fronts. Its initiatives and issues covered include the criminal justice system, the economy, education, guns and crime, health care, immigration, and poverty, to name a few. When it comes to health care, one of its main focus is high prescription drug costs.

Citizens Against Government Waste
1100 Connecticut Avenue, NW, Suite 650
Washington, DC 20036
(202) 467-5300
email: webmaster@cagw.org
website: http://www.cagw.org/

Citizens Against Government Waste is a non-profit and nonpartisan organization that represents more than one million people nationwide in eliminating waste, mismanagement and inefficiency within the government. Among the various issues the organization covers, health care, and prescription drugs costs, are at the forefront.

Fair Pricing Coalition
website: https://fairpricingcoalition.org

The Fair Pricing Coalition is a group that advocates for lower drug prices for HIV and hepatitis drugs. Its website states that it works to ensure that price increases for these drugs don't affect a patient's ability to pay for the drugs. One of the FPC's missions is to negotiate drug prices with pharmaceutical manufacturers to set fair prices for drugs.

The Hastings Center
21 Malcolm Gordon Road
Garrison, NY 10524-4125
(845) 424-4040
email: mail@thehastingscenter.org
website: http://www.thehastingscenter.org/

The Hastings Center was founded in 1969 and is the world's first bioethics research institute. As a non-profit and nonpartisan organization, The Hastings Center has experts from various disciplines who produce everything from books to journals to help inform public understanding of various issues. One of the main initiatives the Center addresses is health care, including prescription drug costs and insurance coverage gaps.

National Coalition On Health Care Action Fund
1111 14th Street NW, Suite 900
Washington, DC 20006
(202) 638-7151
email: CSRxP@csrxp.org
website: http://www.csrxp.org/

The National Coalition On Health Care Action Fund is non-profit organization whose goal is to attain affordable health care for patients. The organization created a separate initiative, called the campaign for Sustainable RX Pricing, which encourages people to educate themselves on high drug costs and learn about how they can help to lower them. The organization's website states that it represents more than 100 million Americans.

Patients For Affordable Drugs
(202) 734-7555
website: http://www.patientsforaffordabledrugs.org

Patients For Affordable Drugs is an independent national patient organization that exclusively focuses on achieving policy changes to lower prescription drug costs. The website serves as a community where patients can tell their stories and make their voices heard on the issue. The organization was founded by patients, David and Nicole Mitchell, who grew tired of high prescription costs.

Physicians for a National Health Program
29 E Madison Suite 1412
Chicago, IL 60602
(312) 782-6006
email: info@pnhp.org
website: http://www.pnhp.org/

Physicians for a National Health Program is a non-profit organization made up of more than 20,000 health professionals across the US. Founded in 1987, the organization's main goal is to advocate for a single-payer national health program. PNHP believes that this type of health program would provide low medical coverage for all Americans.

RxRights
2550 University Ave W, Ste 350 S
Saint Paul, Minnesota, MN 55114
(866) 703-5442
email: advocate@rxrights.org
website: http://www.rxrights.org/

RxRights is a national non-profit that is dedicated to raising awareness about high drug prices. The organization aims to educate the public and the government on the issues facing consumers who depend on prescription drugs. The organization also serves as a forum for consumers to share their stories and opinions on why affordable drug pricing is needed in America.

Bibliography of Books

John Abramson. *Overdosed America: The Broken Promise of American Medicine*. New York, NY: HarperCollins, 2013.

Donald Barr. *Introduction to U.S. Health Policy: The Organization, Financing, and Delivery of Health Care in America*. Baltimore, MD: The Johns Hopkins University Press, 2011.

Kamal Biswas. *Pharma's Prescription: How the Right Technology Can Save the Pharmaceutical Business*. Cambridge, MA: Academic Press, 2013.

Steven Brill. America's Bitter Pill: Money, Politics, Backroom Deals, and the Fight to Fix Our Broken Healthcare System. New York, NY: Random House, 2015.

Ramon Castellblanch. *Driving Down the Cost of Drugs: Battling Big Pharma in the Statehouse*. FirstForum Press, 2011.

Jonathan Dickson and Amy Woebler. *Prescription Drug Pricing: Cost and Control Concerns*. Hauppauge, NY: Nova Science Publishers, 2011.

Joseph Dumit. *Drugs for Life: How Pharmaceutical Companies Define Our Health*. Durham, NC: Duke University Press, 2012.

Insurance Insider. *Hooked: The Rising Cost of Prescription Drugs, and What You Can Do About It*. 2012.

Jeffrey Lobosky. *It's Enough to Make You Sick: The Failure of American Health Care and a Prescription for the Cure*. Lanham, MD: Rowman & Littlefield Publishers, 2012.

Kant Patel and Mark E. Rushefsky. *Healthcare Politics and Policy in America*. Armonk, NY: M.E. Sharpe, 2014.

Gloria R. Pattinson. *Medicare's Prescription Drug Program: Competition Issues and Cost Trends*. Hauppauge, NY: Nova Science Publishers, 2014.

Elisabeth Rosenthal. *An American Sickness: How Healthcare Became Big Business and How You Can Take It Back*. New York, NY: Penguin Press, 2017.

U. S. Government Accountability Office. *Health Care: Programs to Control Prescription Drug Costs Under Medicaid and Medicare Could Be Strengthened*. Columbus, OH: BiblioGov, 2013.

Index